The Guilt-free Book for Pastors' Wives

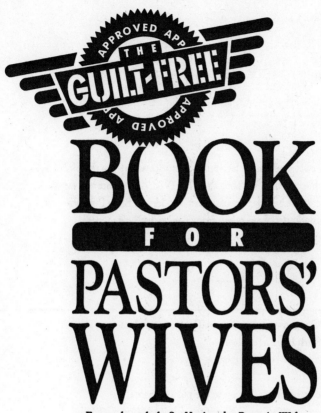

THE
APPROVED APP
GUILT-FREE
APPROVED APP

BOOK

FOR

PASTORS'
WIVES

Formerly titled: *So You're the Pastor's Wife*

RUTH SENTER

VICTOR BOOKS®

A DIVISION OF SCRIPTURE PRESS PUBLICATIONS INC.
USA CANADA ENGLAND

Library of Congress Cataloging-in-Publication Data
    Senter, Ruth Hollinger, 1944-
        The guilt-free book for pastors' wives.

        Revised edition of: So you're the pastor's wife.
        1. Clergymen's wives. 2. Senter, Ruth Hollinger, 1944-
    I. Title.
    BV4395.S45   1990   253'.2   90-12019
    ISBN: 0-89693-798-4

1 2 3 4 5 6 7 8 9 10   Printing/Year 94 93 92 91 90

CONTENTS

PREFACE

So this is what it's like, I thought to myself as I stared blankly at the four bare walls and the six bunk beds lined up in a row. The sleeping bag next to mine was empty. It had been empty since six that morning, and the hands of my travel alarm were almost at midnight now. That wonderful young man who recently had vowed to walk by my side through life had spent a total of five minutes by my side that day, and those five precious minutes had been detached formalities. The wheels of his mind were traveling over the route for the rest of the day. After all, he was in charge; the success or failure of camp depended on his commitment to his job.

I read the same page in my book over for the fifth time and strained my ears to hear the sound of footsteps. I heard nothing but silence. "Someone needs to talk," was all he had said as he hurried away after the evening meeting. *This is God's work,* I thought. *I should be serving with gladness. This is what I have always dreamed of doing—ministering side by side with the man I love, willingly giving and sharing with others.*

It had all looked so beautiful a few short months ago. We would ride off into the sunset with a clergy sticker on the bumper of our car, and hand in hand my minister and I would give ourselves to the work of the Lord.

But sunset had faded into one bare light bulb and six empty bunk beds. I never thought someone might need Mark at midnight, or that people and details would crowd me out of his day. I never thought I would be spending my nights reading a

7

book alone in a cabin with one overhead light bulb for comfort.

This is it. This is what marriage to a pastor is like. The thought hit me in the face like a bucket of cold water. I'd always run from buckets of cold water before, but this time I knew there would be no running, even though I wanted to.

What about me? Where do I fit into all this? He did marry me. I stared at the bare light bulb. I had saved him a seat at lunch, and he never showed. He had been totaling the registration money for the camp manager. Eating was not one of his priorities for the moment. Evidently I wasn't either.

I turned off the light, glad that no one could see my thoughts. None of the pastors' wives I knew would mind reading books in bed alone at midnight. They smiled and were sweet and never seemed to feel resentful when people crowded in on their husbands. They would not mind overhead light bulbs and a row of six bare bunk beds. They would gladly sacrifice for the sake of the ministry.

I pulled my down-filled sleeping bag close around me. It was one way to bury my guilt. I listened for footsteps and heard the lonely sounds of the crickets. I was still feeling the cold water splashing in my face. This was it. For better or for worse.

* * *

Between that lonely light bulb over empty bunk beds and now, a story has been lived. It is my own. It is a story without an ending because it is a story in process. It is not a how-to-do-it story, but a tale of honest struggles. It is about being human. And it is bound together by the divine—the unconditional love—of God for His child.

By telling you my story, perhaps I can hold your hand where you are. Perhaps I can share with you where others are or have been. Hopefully, I can walk with you into some new and undiscovered territory of your life.

Overhead light bulbs becoming sunsets? Rows of empty bunk beds becoming opportunities for rest? Lonely cricket sounds becoming a nocturnal symphony? That's what the struggles of life are all about. That's what the struggles of this book are all about.

And when all is said and done, what really matters is not to whom we are married or what roles we happen to fill in life, but how we respond to the life that God has set before us. Herein lies the thread that draws us together as wives in the process of learning godlike responses to the tension points of life.

So take this book, not as a standard or a model—life is much too unpredictable for that. But take it as an exploration, like one would choose a path never before traveled. These pages are not intended as my performance, for you the spectator to view from afar. They are, rather, intended as a journey to be taken together—writer and reader bonded by experience. I hope this story will not be mine alone, but yours as well. Read my story, then write your own. Paint your own scenes. Fill in your own details. No two journeys are the same. Concentrate on the significance of *your* story. Where have you been, where are you going and where, by God's grace, do you intend to go? If this book can facilitate such exploration, I will feel it has accomplished my intent.

In your quiet moments, you may choose to use the book for personal reflection. At the end of each chapter I have included opportunity for private response. What experiences have these pages brought to your mind? What emotions aroused? What questions raised? What thoughts ignited? What challenges set forth?

For example, when did it first dawn on you that you were a one-of-a-kind pastor's wife, created like no other and free to be like no other? Review the time and place. What else was happening around you? Describe your thoughts, your feelings, before and after. How and when did you see the grace of God break through on behalf of your loneliness, resentment, jealousy, fears, disappointments? Which of God's lessons would you pass on to other pastors' wives for the rekindling of their hope?

For this sisterhood in which we find ourselves needs the offering of hope to one another. The journey alone will most surely end in despair; taken together, in strength. For where one is weak, others can nourish. When one stumbles, others can steady. So then, don't let your story end with you. Pass it on. God's miracles of hope are always worth passing on. When you pass them on, two things happen. First, you are forced to review. And second, you are forced to conclude. Conclusions about God's grace spent on your behalf in the past always lead to hope for today and tomorrow. And when you look back upon the miracles of grace in your life, then humbly offer them to another as reinforcement for their bedraggled soul, you are passing along hope as surely as if you had offered a bowl of hot soup to a hungry stomach on a cold winter's night.

At the end of each chapter you will find, not only opportunity for private reflection, but opportunity for offering hope to another through the use of discussion guidelines. Perhaps you will use the guidelines in a classroom or seated in a circle at a monthly get-together of pastors' wives, or one-on-one, across a cup of coffee with the pastor's wife down the block.

Sometimes you will not want to read about being a pastor's wife. It may be enough simply to live it. Read about it anyhow. Sometimes you may not want to talk about being a pastor's wife. You feel you have nothing to say. Talk about it anyhow. Sometimes you may feel you have nothing hopeful about being a pastor's wife to offer anyone. Offer it anyhow.

As you read, talk, offer, you may find yourself in the process of restoring hope. For even when your supply of hope is depleted, and you have nothing to give your fellow pastor's wife but your poor deplorable self, you may be giving her the best gift of all, for you may be giving her the opportunity to review and draw conclusions about the miracles of grace in her own life. She may rise to hope so as to have something to offer you for your despair. Such is what sisterhood is all about—giving to each other when we are weak *and* giving when we are strong. Such is what the intent of this book is all about.

It is also my intent that as you read, privately reflect, and publicly respond, you will think less about what you should be doing that you are not doing and focus more on God's affirmations of grace in your life. How has He comforted you through His Word—your daily bread? When has He touched your life through another person? When has He given to you through another's gift? When have you looked into another's face and seen lines of His own gentleness and strength? When did you feel His care through another's expression of care for you?

The amazing consequence of dwelling on and in the love of God is that the more we think on it the less inclined we are to try to earn it. We need not be frantic for approval. We already are approved. We need not set lofty expectations for ourselves. He is not disappointed in us. When He looks at us, He sees us through His beloved Son. We are not in the hole, trying to climb out. We are already out, lifted up by His gracious cross of love. God is love. God is in the process of moving us toward divine love, not of keeping score of how much we have or have *not* done for Him.

There is no reason to read this book and feel guilty, for this is a story, as are all stories, not of perfection, but of process. When we admit to process we have every reason to feel hopeful, for the final chapter is never written. We turn the page with each new day, and we find new mercies of grace.

ONE

It's What's Up Front That Counts—or Is It?
Learning to Know Myself

The day wasn't particularly hot, but I could feel myself melting. The sight in front of me made my mouth go dry. I tried to focus on the stained-glass windows and forget the crowd. "Why did I ever say yes?" I lamented as I eyed the red exit signs on either side of the platform. There would be no exit now; the organist had begun her somber tune. My gaze shifted to the grief-stricken faces before me.

"A pastor's wife must be prepared for anything," one of the pastoral staff had remarked lightly as he handed me the list of songs the family wanted sung at the funeral. "You were in glee club in college. You'll do fine." And he hurried off to attend to other details of the service.

Me! The soloist for a funeral? I had never had a voice lesson in my life. I couldn't even sing harmony unless I was standing next to someone who was. But there I sat, in one of those solemn, high-backed chairs between my husband and the senior pastor, staring out over an audience that wanted to hear a song.

The rest of that service was one big blur to me. I don't remember how I ever sang. I do remember a mouth as dry as Utah's salt flats and breathing that came in short, heavy puffs. How I ever got a song through that obstacle course, I'll never know, but somehow I did. I had to. I do remember using a different exit the next Sunday morning because I was too embarrassed to face the organist who normally exited at the same door I did.

Who was Ruth Senter that day? Outwardly, she was a versatile young pastor's wife who could fit into any niche in the church program at a moment's notice. Inwardly, she was a frightened child who was saying, "No, I don't want to be embarrassed in front of all these people. I really don't know how to sing. Please, may I leave?"

Why do we ascend platforms that are not our kind of platforms, or sit in chairs that don't fit us, or sing songs when we should be reading poetry? As I look back upon my first and last vocal solo, I suspect that it was much easier for me to perform as other people expected me to perform than it was to determine what really was for me and what was not me. I had never taken personal inventory, so I wasn't sure what was in my store. Consequently, I tried to merchandise something I really didn't possess. I acted according to someone's expectations and not according to the internal resources God had given me.

It is far easier to live life by memorizing a list or by allowing others to tell us what to do. Things are a lot tougher when we assume the responsibility for making our own choices, and when we base those choices on a proper evaluation of ourselves—our abilities, our limitations, our attitudes, our values, our temperaments.

I have the feeling that many times we don't get around to being loving, kind, gentle, patient, peaceful, confident, honest, etc., because we are too busy worrying about what we should do. Thus, activity, rather than character becomes the gauge for our spirituality, and outward performances become more important than inward conditions.

People seemed to have the same problem in Jesus' day. In fact, the Pharisees were so busy polishing up the externals while neglecting the things of the heart, that Jesus said of them, "These people honor me with their lips but their hearts are far from me. They worship in vain; their feelings are but rules taught by men" (Mark 7:6-7). He advised them to first take care of the inside and then the outside would take care of itself (Matt. 23:26).

What does taking care of the inside involve? It involves a thought process: making the conscious choices in our daily routines that will bring about godlike qualities; cultivating the fruit of the Spirit which God has made available to us—love, joy, peace, patience, kindness, goodness, faithfulness, gentleness, self-control (Gal. 5:22-23); thinking through the opportunities that will best utilize the gifts and abilities God has given us; being aware of our potential, our limitations, and our emotional makeup.

A wise servant knows what to do with the goods his master has given to him. Jesus made this point in one of His parables (Matt. 25). Knowing what to do with myself includes knowing who I am: what are my interests, my abilities, my goals, my dreams, my hopes, my fears, my strengths, and my weaknesses? Knowing what kind of person I am helps me define my roles in life.

"Who is Ruth Senter?" a friend once asked me. I was uncomfortable with the question. After all, I had more important things to do than to think about who I was. My friend knew me. She knew whose wife I was, who my children were, where I lived, how I decorated my house, where I shopped, where I went to eat.

Wasn't that enough? Why the "Who is Ruth Senter?" She sounded as if we were strangers, when we had known each other for several years.

I was asked the same thing just recently, but this time at least I understood the question. It concerned the internals rather than the externals. Somewhere between the two questions, my emphasis had begun to move inward. I'd begun to realize that the Christian life is not performing; it is being. It is not filling a role or playing a part, but responding to life offstage and out of the glare of the lights.

Moving the emphasis inward does not mean becoming a self-centered person, but a self-understanding person. What have I always assumed myself to be? Is that accurate? Is that how things really are, or simply how I'd like them to be? In what have I succeeded? Where have I failed? What do I enjoy? How do I respond to people? How do I learn most effectively? How do I work most effectively? How do I relax most effectively? What are the most important things in life to me? What kinds of people do I enjoy the most? When do I get uptight? What makes me cry? What do I want to accomplish in my lifetime?

Inventories and examinations are never easy, but they are necessary because they tell us the truth about the present and allow us to make plans for the future. They help us define who we are, rather than dictate how to fill our roles.

Discovering how to be the person God designed us to be often comes about through trial and error. For example, I remember how surprised I was to come to the conclusion that working with children was not my particular niche in life, when I had always assumed it was.

My mother was a pastor's wife. She was also a good children's worker, and still is. She has taught Good News Clubs for years.

She speaks at children's rallies and teacher-training classes. If there are children to be taught, she teaches them.

My mother's niche seemed a natural niche for me too. What church didn't need people who were willing to work with children? It was a good way for a pastor's wife to plug in. So I took notes from Mother with great fervor, assuming I would absorb some of her proficiency. I collected materials, built files, bought puppets and magic tricks, cut, pasted, colored, read children's magazines and magazines about how to work with children. I came up with all kinds of creative ideas.

Then one day someone asked me to teach a class of adults. I was startled by the possibility. I had never thought of myself in that particular role, but I cautiously took the assignment. To my amazement, I enjoyed teaching that Sunday School class. I also enjoyed going home without my regular Sunday high-intensity headache. I even found myself looking forward to teaching the class again the following Sunday. My two-week assignment with the adult class stretched into eight weeks and an invitation to return again the next quarter.

I began to consider that there might be an option to coloring, pasting, cutting, and drawing. I wasn't particularly gifted in arts and crafts, and even folding on a dotted line was a gigantic job for me. The discipline end of working with young children didn't come easily either. I never knew what to do with, "But, teacher, you called on her last time." Having to break in on the life of Moses to separate the troublemakers or intercept a paper airplane usually affected my tranquillity for the rest of the day.

But I did feel comfortable outlining a course on Bible study methods for adults. I was stimulated by the interaction; I enjoyed asking questions and listening to answers. Preparing overhead transparencies and mimeographed outlines seemed to take much less time than putting together shadow boxes or cutting out flannelgraph figures. I began to realize that I was a much more relaxed, efficient, and happy person when I was teaching adults.

Were those years of pouring all my energies into working with children a waste of time? No. Those experiences give me the conviction to say no when I'm asked to head a primary department in Vacation Bible School or teach a first-grade Sunday School class. It took those years of working with children to make me realize that that particular area is not God's design for me.

God isn't out to stuff us into a mold that doesn't fit. He doesn't expect us to counterfeit resources because of whose wife we happen to be or because of what we think others are expecting from us. God gives the gifts, but He leaves it up to us to discover what His gifts are. That discovery may involve some trial-and-error experiences, but these experiences can teach us much about ourselves.

It is also interesting to see how much we can learn about ourselves from other people. To see ourselves through someone else's eyes can be a valuable aid in the process of discovering who we are, for self-discovery does not occur in isolation.

I had a professor for a time management class once who suggested that we each choose a personal board of directors to act as a mirror and a sounding board for us. I liked my prof's suggestion and decided to try it. My board of directors is simply three or four friends whose insight I value and respect. I plan lunch with each of them several times a year just for the purpose of asking for their opinions, advice, and ideas.

Sometimes a trusted friend can help us see strengths and weaknesses we are unable to see because we are too close to ourselves. It was a friend who encouraged me to try writing. Another friend made the observation to me one day that I tended to be a perfectionist who needed to learn to relax some of my unrealistic standards for myself. Trying to see myself as others see me has taught me some important things about myself and about the gifts God has or has not given me.

Jesus had His own personal board of directors, too. They were twelve in number. He did not hesitate to ask His disciples, "Who do people say that the Son of man is?" or "Who do you say that I am?" (Matt. 16:13, 15) Jesus probably asked those questions as much for the benefit of His disciples, but the point is that He drew upon the opinions and insights of others concerning matters of His identity.

God has created us with the ability to feel, to think, to choose, to do. Knowing ourselves includes knowing how we function in all four areas. Giving thought to who we are is not necessarily an ego trip. Rather, it can be a process that frees us from ourselves and allows us to be consistent with the person God designed us to be.

Knowing and admitting that you may function better in a place or position other than your present niche is not an invitation to cop out. It is not a license for laziness or selfishness. The issue is not whether I will serve but how I will serve (leading discussions, baking brownies, heading a worship committee, washing communion cups, editing the church magazine, taking an eighty-year-old grocery shopping) and whom I will serve (family, friends, Sunday School class, adults, children, other pastors' wives, senior citizens). As a Christian, I cannot bypass service. As a human, I cannot exist without roles in which to function. So then, my self-assessment becomes a guide for how best I may serve and function, not a determinant for whether or not I will.

Life does not always give me the luxury of choice. Some things must be done simply because they are there for the doing and no one else is available to do them. It is then that the fruit of the Spirit spoken of earlier (love, joy, peace, patience, kindness, faithfulness, gentleness, self-control) can provide supernatural reinforcement for my natural deficiencies. If, for example, I am not completely at ease with two-year-olds but there is no one else to staff the nursery for the four Sunday nights of November, I can count on the grace of God to provide peace to see me through the challenge at hand. God's spirit is given to help me do what I cannot otherwise do for myself. "It's beyond my comfort level," is never enough reason to turn my back on the occasional emergency needs that life may call on me to meet from time to time.

If however, I do have a choice about which age group I will teach in Sunday School or whether I should be a public speaker or serve on church committees, and if there are others to staff the two-year-old nursery for the four Sunday nights in November, I would do well to take time for personal inventory before saying yes to opportunity. Such action will enable me to set for myself a course of direction that is within the comfort range of what I know and what I am discovering daily about myself.

Taking time for personal inventory may mean I have to plan a time free from distractions. Nothing is quite so distraction-free as a retreat center where quiet reflection and prayer are the only business of the day. God has opportunity to be heard. I have opportunity to hear. It is in the hearing of that still, small voice that I often find my focus—my sense of identity, my sense of direction.

For the Christian, the quest to understand oneself is never an end in itself. My focus inward must always lead to a focus outward and upward, otherwise I become an emotional miser—always set on preserving and protecting myself. Such is not the pattern for service. Such is not the route to contentment. On the other hand, when I know my strengths and weaknesses, my abilities and my disabilities, and when I am expressing myself accordingly, there will be a sense of well-being to my life. True, I will have my moments of chaos and confusion—"What am I doing in this job?" or "Is this how I really want to spend the rest of my life?" But apart from occasional lapses, the pattern of my life will be a calm assurance that I am living out God's blueprint for my life.

* * *

Interaction Time
Personal Reflection

1. If someone were to ask me, "Who are you, really?" I would answer. . . .

2. I am usually not able to answer such questions because. . . .

3. If someone had never met me and I were writing a description of myself for them, I would write. . . .

4. If I had to quantify how well I feel I know myself, on a scale of one to ten, I would rate myself. . . .
I gave myself the above rating because . . .

5. If I had to quantify my feelings of contentment and self-acceptance, on a scale of one to ten, I would rate myself. . . .
I gave myself the above rating because. . . .

6. If I had to quantify the confidence and peace I have about how I am investing my time and energies, on a scale of one to ten, I would rate myself. . . .
I gave myself the above rating because. . . .

7. I feel uncertain and insecure about myself when. . . .

8. The times I feel most certain and secure are. . . .

9. What do my answers to 7 and 8 tell me about myself?

10. From God's perspective, I am. . . . (List Scriptural references.)

11. From God's perspective, I can . . . (List Scriptural references.)

12. One new thought about myself that has come as a result of this exercise is. . . .

13. One further step of self-discovery I need to take is. . . .

14. My thoughts to God on the matter of self-discovery are. . . .

* * *

Group Interaction
1. Do you agree or disagree with the line of reasoning that goes, "A Christian should not be bothered about self-discovery. Service is primary. As one serves, she will discover herself."

2. Granted that self-discovery is a healthy exercise, how does one keep self-discovery from becoming morbid introspection?

3. What clues does one have that self-analysis may be becoming unhealthy?

4. Do you think pastors' wives have a greater struggle with personal identity than other women? Why or why not?

5. What particular exercise or discipline has been helpful to you in your process of learning to understand yourself?

6. Is there a person who has been particularly helpful to you

in the process? What did that person do for you?

7. What Scripture or biblical principle has been helpful to you in the process?

8. What advice would you give to someone who says, "I don't have a clue who I am or why I'm doing the things I'm doing."

9. What would you ask God to do for the person who is especially struggling with self-understanding?

TWO

"How to" in Twelve Easy Lessons
Learning to Cope with Roles

"If you could give everyone in this room a character gift, what would your gifts be?"

We all sat there in embarrassed silence. It wasn't as though we were strangers to each other. It was the last night of a three-week missionary trip to Mexico, and we had agonized together under some pretty heavy loads. For three weeks we had been a family, and you get to know each other quite well when you are a family.

For three weeks I had struggled to balance my roles with my family of sixteen. I had many hats, and they weren't all Mexican sombreros. I was wife, companion, substitute mother, cook, counselor, friend, nurse, and chauffeur, all wrapped into one.

It wasn't that I minded all my hats. But something seemed to be pulling me in a million different directions during that trip. I wasn't sure what it was until someone put her finger on it as we passed out our character gifts to each other at the end of our trip.

"I give to Ruth the ability to be the same person no matter who she is around." I questioned my gift-giving analyst further. "When you're around us, you come across as a confident person. When you were around the missionaries, you played the humble role and were really down on yourself. When you are around me, you seem to be a person with your own thoughts. When you are around Mark, you change. I'm never sure who you really are."

I was reminded of the chameleons we used to have around our cotton farm in southern Alabama when I was growing up. You never knew when you were seeing the same chameleon. If he was on a green leaf, he was green. When he crawled onto a brown tree trunk, he turned brown. I was sure that if I could ever catch him and put him on my pink sweater, he would turn pink.

I thought a lot about my gift after that night; it was one of the most valuable gifts I've ever received. I also thought a lot about the hats I wear—pastor's wife, friend, mother, writer, neighbor, daughter. I decided that hats are functional. They are not worn to disguise me, to make me someone I am not, or to change my personality. Life calls for different hats in just the same way that one person may play different roles in a dramatic production. However, my perceptive teenage friend saw in me not just one actress switching roles, but one person trying to be more than one actress. It wasn't just a change of roles; it was a change of person.

Although life calls for many changes of hats, the person under the hat is far more important than the hat itself. It is when I change as a person, depending on which hat I'm wearing, that I've lost sight of who I really am. It's when I make the hat my whole person that the true me gets covered up.

My role as a pastor's wife is not all there is of me. It is a very important hat that I wear, but it is not the only one. The same is true of my roles as mother, daughter, sister, friend, teacher, writer. They are my functions in life. They are the parts God's script has assigned me. But they are not my identity. My external functions are not the internal me. My personality, my temperament, my attitudes, my feelings are the real me. Who I am is what God has given me. My roles are what I choose to do with those gifts.

My identity does not change when I plug into different outlets of life, even though my mood might change. Sometimes I'm sad; sometimes I'm happy. I may be talkative one day and quiet and pensive the next. Some days I feel carefree, while other days I'm intense. Moods change. Roles change. Who I am should not.

Perhaps it is time to remove our role hats and take a good look at the person under the hat. Perhaps it is time we allow what we are to determine how we function rather than allowing how we function to determine what we are. The solution is not to forget roles, but to be the person God designed us to be. Only then will we know what to do with the functions that life calls us to fill.

One of the most effective pastors' wives I know is a woman whom I have never heard speak in terms of her role as pastor's wife. Yet she is loved and respected by her husband's congregation. She appears to understand her life, to be content with her life, and to have figured out her gifts and given them to the body of Christ. She also knows her limitations and lives within those boundaries.

I was privileged to be able to observe her for a period of time as a member of her household. I saw a woman who was in private what she was in public. She knew what to do with her roles in life because she knew what to do with herself, and thus, her roles were a logical extension of who she was. They were uniquely her own. She was not simply an extension of her roles.

How did my effective friend arrive at the place where she was free not to agonize over her role as pastor's wife? Probably at some stage in her growth and development she had agonized. A fear that is never faced is the fear that may someday overwhelm us.

Roles that are never thought through may be the roles that bury us.

My own struggle with being a pastor's wife took me through the how-to-do-it stage. We had not been married a month when I pulled out my book on how to be a good wife. I had taken copious notes on the book before we were married, but somehow the theories which had looked so good on paper weren't working. I reread. I formed mental pictures of the wife of the book and carried the images around in my brain; I memorized them just as I had memorized French vocabulary cards in school.

And I bought more books: books on how to be a pastor's wife, how to entertain, how to keep your mate happy, how to live on fifteen dollars a week or less, how to cook "interesting" casseroles. I knew things would be so simple if I could just find the right formula. So I swallowed my how-to-do-it vitamins and waited for them to take effect.

But I kept encountering the exceptions. Mark was not always predictable. People in the church didn't always respond right. My casseroles didn't look like the pictures in the book. I didn't always feel the way the book said I should feel. I followed all the recipes, but extra ingredients kept popping up in my life—ingredients that the recipes didn't call for.

When you live life from a book, it is hard to know what to do with the unpredictables. Sometimes there is no one there to tell you what to do, and you have to decide for yourself. That can be a frightening experience.

I've always been fascinated by the way Jesus dealt with people. He wanted them to learn certain things about life and godliness, but He didn't publish a handbook or conduct a seminar on "how to be a disciple in twelve easy lessons." He didn't monitor their every move or have them turn in weekly progress reports. He taught principles and then trusted His disciples to apply those principles to life. Perhaps He knew that following a manual would be an easy solution to life's perplexities but that easy solutions aren't always the best solutions.

Another stage in my role struggle was the how-they-do-it stage. I took my cues from what other pastors' wives did. Now there is a fine line between learning from someone else and taking on their personality, and it took me awhile to see the difference. I would talk with a pastor's wife who would inspire me, and I would come home a different person. I would attend a seminar, and I would change. I would remember how Mother did it, and I would become Mother. I was learning a lot about other people but very little about myself.

How-they-do-it is not all wrong. There are times when we need someone who knows what it's like to be a pastor's wife; when we need a model and an example; when we need the wisdom of years from someone who has been there. Knowing how they do it can encourage, stimulate, and teach.

But how-they-do-it can also destroy us if we let it. I can remember coming home with an overwhelming sense of how I was not doing it after talking with a young pastor's wife. I had asked her all kinds of questions about how she had adjusted to life in the parsonage. She seemed pleased that I asked and gave me glowing accounts. I came home convinced that she had her act perfectly together. What was taking me so long? I suddenly felt terribly inadequate.

A preoccupation with how-they-do-it can also keep us from asking the crucial question—How should I do it? For years after Mark and I were married, we went everywhere together. When he had a speaking engagement, a camp, or a retreat, I was always a part. However, things were considerably more complex with two children on the scene.

It was Wisconsin's coldest month—February—and Mark was to be one of the speakers at a winter retreat. Nicky was only nine months old, so I decided not to go. A winter retreat was not the place for a nine-month-old who was very susceptible to colds and ear infections; at least that's what I thought until I heard that the wife of one of the speakers was going and taking her two children. And her baby was even younger than Nicky. Then I decided that maybe there were some reasons why I should go. I bundled everyone up, and we headed north to the cold woods.

It took our family four weeks to get over that retreat. We went from infection to infection. I lay in bed and stared at the ceiling for seven days while I tried to catch my breath through a maze of bronchial congestion. I talked to myself a good bit during those seven days. I didn't have enough voice to talk to anyone else! One of the things I said to myself during that time was that it didn't matter how anyone else did it. What mattered was how the Senter family should do it.

Why I disobeyed my better instincts and went to that retreat, I'm not sure. But in all honesty, it was probably because I wasn't prepared to have another pastor's wife rate a higher score than me on dedication, loyalty, and sacrifice. Going on a winter retreat with a small baby was sure proof of all three.

I always liked to win elections in high school, and college too. It assured me that I was doing something just a little better than someone else. When there weren't any more high school or college elections to win, I found my competition in other ways. When I'm in competition with someone, their actions become the basis for what I do. When I'm being myself, I can enjoy others, learn from them, but take the course of action I feel God would have me take, regardless of what they do.

Sometimes we take the how-they-think-I-should-do-it route to determine our course of action. We take great pains to read our audience. What do they expect from us? What do they want to see in us? What do they want to hear from us? These questions can be meaningful if they make us more sensitive to where our audience is, but if they determine which speech we will give, we've become a robot and someone else is pushing our controls. Living by the standards other people have set for us makes us actors. It fragments our lives, because no two standards for us are the same. We become all things to all people and lose ourselves in the shuffle.

Living the way we assume other people think we should live can be exhausting. Mark and I had just returned from a speaking engagement. It had been a grueling schedule, and I was tired. But that night there was to be a bridal shower for the daughter of one of the leading families in the church. I felt people would expect me to be there. So I swallowed two aspirin, brushed out the wrinkles from the two-hour plane ride, and joined the celebration just in time to see the first gift opened.

The interesting thing about the evening was that no one had expected to see me there. I even surprised the bride. If I heard it once, I heard it a dozen times: "We didn't expect you to be here. You must have just gotten in from your trip."

I had misread my audience. I had missed my cue. And so I sat with blurry eyes and watched the mountain of wrapped gifts disappear and tried to carry on a sane conversation. Everyone else had expected me to be home in bed, and there I sat. No one had expected a thing out of me that night; they had been kind to me. That was more than I could say about the way I had treated myself. As I dropped into bed that night, I determined that following my God-given intuition was probably much more sensible than worrying over what others were expecting from me.

What about our roles? How should we handle them? The first step is to understand roles. Roles are society's way of organizing itself, fitting its citizens into functions. We would not be able to operate, or to hand down our culture from one generation to another were it not for roles. We need not therefore look at roles as restrictions or uncomfortable straitjackets, but rather as society's designations.

Roles are the result of our associations in life. We would be about as lifeless as a concrete slab if we did not have the ability to form associations. I'm Mark Senter's wife, Jori Senter's mother, Elam Hollinger's daughter, Nelda Cockman's friend— all roles, all associations from which I draw warmth, love, support, and strength. How I respond to these associations is a logical extension of what I am. It is not a prescribed formula or a role play. Instead, it is a genuine expression of all that makes up *me*—my abilities, my personality, my emotions, my background.

I do not go out of my way to meet people at church because I am Mark's wife, or Jori's mother, or Elam's daughter, or Nelda's friend. I do it because it comes naturally. That's how God mixed my chemistry. I do not teach the young adult class in Sunday School because I'm Mark's wife, or Jori's mother, or Elam's daughter, or Nelda's friend. I teach because I enjoy teaching young adults and feel it is a gift God has given me to use.

"There are different kinds of gifts . . . of service . . . of work-ing," Paul says (1 Cor. 12:4-6). Diversity is one of the strengths of the body of Christ. Why should we try to make ourselves into duplicates of one another by following formulas when that is not what God has in mind for His body, the church?

In Ephesians 2:10 Paul calls believers God's "workmanship." The word Paul uses is the Greek word *poiema* from which we get our English word "poem." Each of us is one of God's literary pieces, and He is making a statement through us. We cannot change the meter, the lyrics, or the title, and no two poems are ever used in exactly the same way or have exactly the same effect. That's what keeps the body of Christ alive and exciting.

When it comes to being comfortable with my roles, it is important I recognize that just as there are many gifts in the body of Christ, so there are many ways to fulfill one particular role. While society assigns certain behavior codes to its citizens, within the codes there is wide room for variety. Focusing on the unlimited possibilities for fulfilling a particular role frees one from feeling restricted. The focus must always be, "What is the best way for me to fill this particular role?" rather than "How should this role be performed?"

If I am to be at peace with the roles life has assigned me, I must distinguish between my roles and my personhood. Roles are the external me, the "me" others see. My performances, my skills, my activities, my hobbies, my responses to others. My "person" houses the private side of me, my fears, my dreams, my hopes, my pain, my feelings, and thoughts—the parts of me I may give out only to a few select persons. Both sides of me— my roles and my person, need to be acknowledged and nour-ished. If both parts are continually fed, I won't need to fear sacrificing my person to my roles. Instead, I can accept the fact that, yes, life has assigned me a role but yes, I am also a "person," unique, private, selective in dispersement. I will spend as much effort on maintaining positive character traits, dreaming dreams, reflecting on God's word to me as I do learn-ing to lead a small group discussion, overhauling my wardrobe, or taking classes at the local junior college. Both categories are important maintenance exercises. Caring for both types of personal needs means that I am less likely to feel overwhelmed by a role.

Roles need not overwhelm me. They need not be seed for resentment. Instead, when properly understood and accepted they may become the very structure that allows me to function with ease and to be content with the person God created me to be.

Interaction Time
Personal Reflection
1. How do I feel when someone introduces me, "This is . . . , our pastor's wife?"

2. What clue does my response give about how I feel toward my "role" as pastor's wife?

3. If someone would ask me how I define my role as pastor's wife, I would say. . . .

4. What about my role as pastor's wife is difficult for me?

5. What have I done in the past to comfortably fit being a pastor's wife with being myself?

6. If God were speaking directly to me about my roles, I think He might say. . . .

7. Scripture references or biblical principles which might pertain to the issue of roles are. . . .

Group Interaction
1. How would you define the term "role"?

2. Why do you think people in general resist roles? Why do you think pastors' wives in particular resist roles?

3. What suggestions might you make to role resisters?

4. Can you think of a pastor's wife who "was her own

person" and yet graciously fulfilled her role as pastor's wife? Describe the person. What about her seemed to make it possible to do both?

5. Do you agree or disagree that most of us have the tendency to worry more about fulfilling our "roles" than about nurturing our "person." If you agree, why do you think it is true? What might be a more healthy alternative?

6. Where have you struggled most with your role of pastor's wife?

7. How did you overcome?

8. What insights and understanding have you come to about your role as pastor's wife that might be worth passing on to others?

THREE

How Many Times
Does It Take
To Be Good?
Learning to Deal with Failure

It was my first big chance. I had been asked to be the Bible
teacher for senior high camp. I pulled out my notes from my
three years of Bible school and from my communications major
in college. I had it all together when it came to the theories of
communication; I was a capable computer when it came to
biblical knowledge. And so I marched confidently in with my
visual aids and my storehouse of knowledge.

But my academic props hit the floor with a smash. The thing
I had forgotten was that there would be people in my audience.
There would be people who would look at me and say, "I dare
you to teach me something"; who would stare right through me
and out to the lake where there were canoes and rafts and

three-meter diving boards; who would smile sweetly at me while their notes were being passed around the circle. Suddenly the whole scene was one big threat.

The biggest threat of all was the senior pastor's daughter, Sue. In her eyes I saw, "This better be good. I'm taking a full report home to Dad." She had always been my buddy before. She had laughed at my jokes and talked to me about boys, and I had been sure of her approval. Until now. Suddenly things changed. It was as though someone had pushed a huge block of ice between us. I saw no sign of acceptance or approval from Sue or from anyone else in that entire audience. Things were very unsafe.

I looked to the counselors for support. There they sat— pastors, youth workers, college students. Were they smiling or frowning? Was that a nod of approval or were they sleeping? I wished I had double-checked some of my facts. And what about my technique? My topic? Was I anywhere near the teenage wavelength?

Following that morning's Bible hour came a period of pro-longed self-evaluation and introspection. I was a friend to ev-eryone, but was I helpful to anyone? To help people you have to get below the surface, I concluded. On meaningful interac-tion with people, I rated myself about a minus ten.

I was sure that a pastor's wife needed a much higher rating than that—especially one who taught teens at summer camp. I wanted very much to be the kind of person who had people lining up outside her door waiting to unload their feelings. I noticed every counselor there that week who had that kind of rapport with their kids. I also noticed the empty hall outside my door.

I sat in my room and studied or mimeographed neat little worksheets for the next lesson. That was safe. It kept me from people. People were beginning to remind me of what I was not. The block of ice between Sue and me grew to a glacier. Her polite tolerance became what I diagnosed as open hostility. She had her crowd around her; she called the shots. And I felt that her shots were definitely not in my favor.

I took her actions personally and built my line of defense: I became an authority. After all, I was the teacher. Outwardly I came on stronger; inwardly I was shrinking. Before the week was half over I had written my own grade—failure with a capital F.

"What was right about your teaching this morning?" Mark asked me after another of my "I'm blowing it" laments. I couldn't think of anything positive, but I had the negatives memorized.

And of course the reason was Sue. I felt a little better if I could fix the blame on someone else. She was just another of those rebellious preacher's kids who was reacting against her father's busyness. Somewhere along the line he should have spent more time with her. It sure would have made it easier on me.

I thought of all the super speakers who had gotten through to me as a high-schooler. I tried them on for size. I took careful notes on the way teens came to Mark for counsel and advice. I tried to blend into his style.

By the end of the week my self-esteem had shrunk to midget proportions. As a matter of fact, there weren't many things left that I even liked about myself. How I perceived people responding to my morning Bible hour performance had colored my whole life. Not only had I given myself a failing grade as friend and teacher, but I also was gradually writing myself off as a pastor's wife and person. I waited for the approval and listened for the applause, but it never came. I was ready to pack my bags and head for home.

Finally the stakes were so low that I had nothing to lose. I decided to take a risk and called Sue to my room. I never got past "I'm concerned. . . ." The glacier melted into tears. That afternoon Sue and I struggled together with feelings we didn't understand; with what we knew but weren't sure how to apply; with relationships to other people. She was struggling at one stage, I at another. We both laid aside our games and helped each other.

I never did receive a standing ovation for my Bible teaching at camp that year, but eleven years later I received my paycheck.

Sue wrote to me from South America where she is a mission-ary: "Last night we played a game where we had to write down who had had the greatest influence on our lives other than our parents. I remembered that year at camp when you called me to your room. For me that was a turning point. I wrote your name down. I just wanted you to know."

Experience can so often teach us what the books cannot. It is what we consider our failures, or what are in fact failures, that can teach us to dig deeper, to stretch further, to run faster. However, our failures can also become personal tragedies if we let them become the basis for our self-esteem or if they distort our view of reality.

Because we may fail does not necessarily mean we are fail-ures. It is easy to fill our report card with F's if we start with the premise that we are failures. We spend all our time agonizing over our negatives and never get around to building upon our positives. We dwell on all that we are not rather than trust God for all that we could be. It is easy to see God's works of art in everyone but us.

Where does a failure complex come from? There is never a simple answer, but I have some pretty strong clues about myself.

One of the times that I tended to write myself off was when I felt rejected or neglected. Someone was not paying me the attention I thought I deserved. That feeling was generally di-rected toward my on-the-go husband. The times I would feel like I was failing Motherhood 102 were often the days when Mark had committee meetings every night of the week, or had two weddings in one weekend, or had to fly out of town for a couple days.

Now granted, children do have a built-in sonar called "tak-ing advantage" when there is only one parent around. But the interesting thing was that I would often feel in perfect control of the situation until Mark got home. The image of myself that I would project to him when he sat down to hear the good news of the day was often much more devastating than the image I had carried about myself during his absence. What had been just a ripple in my calm would come out as a tidal wave when I rehearsed it to Mark. What had been just a natural human response would come out as a tragic flaw in my character. I would draw all kinds of unfair conclusions about myself.

Why was I so hard on myself in the aftermath of Mark's absence? It was my way of lashing out against his busyness. It was my way of saying, "I'm losing control. You'd better spend more time at home obeying Scripture's command to do a good job managing your own household." I'd never say it. I'd never blame him or the church. No good, loyal pastor's wife would do that. But I sure was great at blaming myself in a way that would make him blame himself. I got the same results.

Sometimes I won my game. We'd go out for dinner, just the two of us, or Mark would spend extra time with the children. However, the taste of victory was always bittersweet. I had won a point, but at the expense of my own self-esteem. I played the failure game to gain the attention I felt I was missing.

Another time I noticed my self-esteem slipping to sub-zero was when I had too much time to dwell on myself—time to think of all I was missing or all I was sacrificing. While I was busy, I generally liked what I was doing and I generally liked myself. However, when I was sitting home from church because Nicky had sneezed that day or the children hadn't gotten their Sunday afternoon naps, I could very easily become a martyr. Mixed in with my martyrdom would be all kinds of unkind thoughts about myself: It doesn't matter whether I'm at church or not. Who needs me as long as they have Mark? Martyr complexes and failure complexes often come as a double dose, and neither is exactly conducive to spreading good cheer and happiness.

Now there's nothing wrong with staying home from church on a Sunday night because the kids have colds, even if you are the pastor's wife. And there's nothing wrong with thinking about yourself. But too much of it at the wrong time can become hazardous to one's health. I've found the difference to be this: if my feelings about myself are healthy to begin with, self-evaluation can make me healthier. If my feelings about myself are on the down side, I'd better move on to other topics or get busy. Activity may easily become a cover-up for facing my real self, but it also can be the best antidote for discouragement.

If I'm fighting a cold, I will not sit in a draft. If I'm fighting discouragement, I will not sit home and think about myself—even if Nicky sneezed three dozen times that day. Being sensitive to my changing moods and treating myself accordingly has saved me from many negative pitfalls.

Another interesting observation about my self-esteem is that it is often the lowest when I expect the most from other people. For example, take what I considered to be one of my most outstanding mother-daughter banquet productions. At least I thought it was outstanding. I had done this one right—staging, lighting, casting. It was all first class. I'm not sure what I expected from the audience in return, but whatever it was, it wasn't there.

I remember going home with a big question mark about my capabilities. It didn't matter if in fact, the production had been good. In my eyes the whole production, and consequently my ability, had been tarnished because the audience didn't respond to the evening and to me in the way I had expected.

It was another one of those mile markers, however, for when the fog of emotions lifted I realized that I could not draw my feelings of self-worth from others. Approval was something I would have to give to myself. People are not predictable. People forget. They are in a hurry. They have other things on their minds. But because people do not always stop and hand me bouquets does not mean that I'm no good; it only means that people are human.

What does God want us to do about our failures? (One of the things that He doesn't want is for us to dwell upon our failures.) "Whatever is true . . . noble . . . right . . . pure . . . lovely . . . praiseworthy . . . think about such things. . . . Put it into practice. And the God of peace will be with you," Paul states in Philippians 4:8-9. To me, the word "practice" implies that thinking positively about myself is something I must discipline myself to do. It is not something God does for me, but He gives me the ability to do it for myself.

Living under the fear of failure is not God's plan for us either; fear of failure can isolate and paralyze. God hasn't given us the spirit of fear (2 Tim. 1:7). Therefore, if we fear failure, we know it is not God's doing but our own. Instead of fear, God has given us self-control.

Sometimes self-control will mean that we refuse to allow negative thoughts about self to remain in our minds. Read the paper, call a neighbor, play the piano—anything that gets our minds off ourselves. Sometimes it may mean that we exercise our brain to try to determine the reason for our feelings of failure or the reason for our failure. Sometimes it means thinking through a plan for avoiding the same mistake in the future. Sometimes it means talking through our feelings about ourselves with a friend or husband. God has given us all that pertains to life and godliness, and that includes the ability to rebound from our failures as a better person rather than to plod along in the slush of self-pity and despair (2 Peter 1:3).

Several months ago I was strolling leisurely through one of my favorite shopping malls. Suddenly something in one of the windows caught my eye. It was I! I stopped to look. (It was safe because no one could tell what I was looking at.)

The sea of people behind me became a blur, and there was Ruth in that window. Out of all those people in the crowd, I saw myself. I saw myself smile. I didn't remember ever having stood in front of a store window smiling at myself except maybe when I was a kid and didn't know any better.

I was almost embarrassed by the fact that there were things in that window reflection that I liked; I wasn't used to thinking about myself in that way. I liked the outfit I was wearing. I liked the way my hair had been cut the week before. But I saw more. I saw my relaxed facial lines, and eyes that were wide awake. I saw a back that was straight and a hand that rested casually on a shoulder bag. And I liked what I saw. I liked what I was at that moment—content, relaxed, confident, happy. "Thank You, Lord," was the mental message I sent as I almost skipped my way through the crowd.

I wish I could say that I've been skipping my way through life ever since. It would be a nice little fairy tale. But living sometimes calls for my grubby clothes. My hair gets messed up. Some days I cultivate deep furrows on my forehead and press my lips firmly together. Some days my eyes fly at half mast, and I clench my hands or wring them nervously. And some days my shoulders sag, and I don't like myself—how I feel, how I act, how I look.

I'm glad I don't always stand around looking at myself in windows. But remembering myself that day helps me remember that there are right things about God's creation in me. And somehow just remembering the *rights* can help to change a lot of the *wrongs*.

Life will always hand me my fair share of failure. It is part of the fallen world in which I live. Mistake-free living is reserved for heaven. There are times I need to remind myself that I am still living this side of heaven and must put up with a broken system—including failure.

Learning to live with failure means I must monitor my expectations for myself. Much as I can program my children for failure if I constantly expect them to fail, so I can program myself for failure by anticipating I will fail even before I've tried. Statements like, "I should have known I'd blow it," or "Why do I always do dumb things like that?" may well mean that I operate in a failure mode. Being aware of thoughts and words that keep me in that mode may well be the first step toward overcoming it.

Sometimes we fail because we expect ourselves to fail. Other times we may fail because we fear success. We have so programmed ourselves to fail that we stay clear of opportunities that might carry us into the winner's circle. I may be fairly certain that I have cast myself into a failure mode when I am convinced that I fail more than I succeed, when I am more comfortable rehearsing to others my failures than giving myself credit for my successes, when my mistakes are followed up with "See, I failed again."

Pinpointing our disposition to fail may be something we, with the resources of God, can do for ourselves. On the other hand, sometimes the roots go so deep we have to have the expert come and dig them out. But dig them out, we must if we are to experience contented, confident living. God never intended that we live out our days, wallowing in the mire of failure. His "abundant life" promises not only salvation, but also daily overcoming—the trademark of success, not failure.

Interaction Time
Personal Reflection

   1. If I listed "major failures of my life" in one column and "major successes in my life" in another, which column would be the longest? What would the length of my lists tell me about myself?

   2. If someone asked me whether I consider myself a failure or a success I would answer. . . .

   3. I fear (failing, succeeding) most. Clues I have that this is true are. . . .

   4. A time in my past when I felt the most like a failure was when. . . .

   5. A time when I felt the most like a success was when. . . .

   6. I still struggle with feeling like a failure when. . . .

   7. The times I feel the most successful are when. . . .

   8. When I fail I. . . .

   9. I feel that the way I cope with failure is (healthy, unhealthy) because. . . .

   10. One step I need to take to better deal with my mistakes is. . . .

   11. If I were talking to God about how I handle failure, I would say. . . .

Group Interaction

   1. Why do we have such a hard time with our failures?

2. Do you think pastors' wives have a harder time than most? If so, why do you think it is true?

3. From God's point of view, failure is. . . .

4. What Scripture passages may help give perspective on failure? (Using a concordance, check out passages dealing with sin, confession, fall, triumph, victory.)

5. A famous person was once asked, "If you had it to do all over again, what would you do differently?" The answer—"I would have failed more often." What do you think the person meant?

6. We sometimes think of failing as "bad," succeeding as "good." Is failing ever good? When and why?

7. If you had to list the benefits of failing, what would you list? What have been some personal benefits for you?

8. What has been the most important lesson you have learned about failure?

9. If you were counseling someone who looks at himself of herself as a failure, what would you say?

10. What or who has been the biggest help to you during a time when you felt like a failure? Why?

FOUR

The Problem with Pedestals
Learning to Admit Humanness

It all started with the English muffins. They didn't smell quite right as I warmed them in the oven. In fact, they smelled like burning rubber. And burning rubber it was: Nicky had found a perfect hiding place for his tennis shoe. Amid the broiled tennis shoe crisis, Jori came wailing from her room. A page had been torn out of her library book, and the book was due today. My three-year-old Nicky had struck again. The morning was one series of tragedies after another. The whole world seemed plotted against my neat little schedule for getting to my weekly Bible study on time.

The dust was still swirling as I loaded my delinquent little son into the car and raced to church, fifteen minutes late, to teach the lesson from Philippians on peace. I could not do it. Instead, out came the account of my whole awful morning. I made no pretense about having handled my situation calmly and rationally. I told them exactly how it was with me that morning. And all was not well.

"It's nice to know you're human," one of the girls remarked to me later that morning as we were having our coffee and doughnuts.

"Was there ever any doubt that I wasn't?" I asked.

"I guess it's just good to see that you get upset too. I don't feel quite so guilty."

Later, I thought about her comment. Had my friend really gotten an unrealistic picture of me? If so, how did it happen? I had never thought in terms of pedestals for people, much less for myself, but that day I did. If people automatically created pedestals for me, I decided I must fight very hard to remain on the ground. If I had created pedestals for myself, I must try harder to be honest about myself and about my own struggles.

I also saw in my friend's comment a plea for someone with whom she could identify, a need for a companion in process, not a completed work of art at which she could wistfully gaze.

I think sometimes we build our own pedestals by not allowing ourselves to be human, or at least not allowing other people to know that we are human. Sometimes we are more concerned with being on exhibit than we are with being on the drawing board of life. Exhibits are for completed works, not for those in process. It is easy to try to shortcut the process because we are not willing to be patient with ourselves, or because we think others will not be patient with us.

Recently I was trying to get to a friend's house for lunch. I ended up going four miles to get two. The road was under construction, and as I sat at the barricade and stewed over the prospect of a four-mile detour, the street department had the gall to say to me in the form of a little yellow sign, "Road under construction. Thank you for your patience." I decided the sign definitely did not apply to me as I turned my car around and headed in the opposite direction.

Road repairs are not completed overnight. Neither are lives.

There is nothing wrong with admitting that we are involved in a process of learning about life and how God would have us live it. Usually the strong can admit their struggles. Perhaps if we were willing to admit that we are still under construction, we would be stronger and a lot more patient with ourselves.

The more I study Scripture, the less I see great spiritual giants who had the pieces of their lives perfectly fit together. Instead, I read about people involved in the intense struggles of a real life—people who learned to draw upon the resources of a divine God. But they had their struggles, and they shared their struggles with others.

I read about a man after God's own heart who laid bare his thoughts and feelings through the Psalms. David was not a mountain-top man, and he made no pretense of being one. He had his rooftop experiences. He blew it in some pretty significant ways. But he knew how to admit his humanness. He knew how to depend upon his God.

Then there was Moses—a man who probably moved more people, despite almost inconceivable odds, than any other leader in history. There was no prophet in all of Israel like Moses "whom the Lord knew face to face" (Deut. 34:10). Yet the story of Moses is the account of a man in process. He was impetuous. He killed first and thought later. He felt inadequate. He wanted to lean on someone else. He had feelings of despair, inadequacy, rejection, anger, worry, fear, exhaustion, and weakness.

Moses had his moments in the sun. He watched the Red Sea close over his enemies. He saw the bread drop from heaven. He had his moments on the mountain. But he also broke the tablets of stone in anger. He struck the rock to show how clever he was, when God had told him just to speak to the rock. His father-in-law had to remind him that he could not run the show alone.

Then I read in my Bible about Job who was righteous and blameless and God-fearing. Yet he sat on his ash heap and wished he had never been born. He was impatient for some answers to his chaotic life. When I read about Job, I see a man who was floundering, trapped, in total despair. Here was a real person with real hurts, and I hurt with him. I ask the same kinds of questions he asked about the justice of God. And sometimes I feel the same kind of isolation from God.

The Bible shows me people in process, and I take heart. They made it—not in the shade, but under a hot, scorching sun. And the more I know about the hot, scorching sun in their lives, the more aware I am of the grace, love, and power of God in their lives—the same God who is still around for me today.

Fairy tales are nice to read as bedtime stories to our children, but they are devastating if we pretend to live them. Everything is not always all right—even for the Christian. People do not live happily ever after—even Christians. Why do we feel we have to keep up the fairy-tale front?

Why do we think we cannot be human? Why can't we admit that our home is a real place where children scream, where milk spills and tennis shoes get broiled in the oven, where mothers have to take two aspirin to calm their jangled nerves, and where fathers get upset because the cord of their new electric hedge trimmer got cut in half.

What's wrong with admitting that this husband and his wife sometimes aren't so sweet to each other. Sometimes he schedules a board meeting on the night she had planned to entertain friends because he didn't write the plans down on his calendar when she told him three weeks earlier. Sometimes he thinks she should go and she thinks she should stay. Sometimes he comes home and wants to talk and feels ignored because she is so involved in the book she is writing or the class she is taking. Let's face it. That's how things sometimes are. So why do we find it so hard to admit?

Perhaps it is because we have set standards for ourselves which are unrealistic and unattainable. We have drawn up blueprints which completely ignore the human element. We've had our spiritual inoculations, and we expect that to take care of all our carnal germs. When the germs do get through our insulated bubble, we are plagued with guilt because we have failed to meet our own specifications.

God allows for our humanness. That's what His cross is all

about. He knew we would blow it sometimes. That's why He said, "If anybody does sin, we have one who speaks to the Father in our defense—Jesus, the Righteous One" (1 John 2:1). Then in almost the same breath John says, "No one who lives in Him keeps on sinning" (1 John 3:6). At first glance it looks like a gross contradiction. However, in the first verse, the word "sin" means acts of sin; in the second, the verb means to practice sin—to "keep on sinning."

In other words, God does not expect us to make sin a way of life—a practice. Knowing God and practicing sin are incompatible. However, knowing God does not mean that we will never commit acts of sin. Knowing God does not immunize us against mistakes. It does not mean our humanness no longer exists. Knowing God means we have the ability to forgive and forget our mistakes because that's what God does with them.

Those who are in Christ Jesus are not under condemnation, Paul states in Romans 8:1. Yet how often we fumble around in the fog of our own guilt because we can't attain the perfect standards we have set. God is in the fog-lifting business; it's called confession and forgiveness. God intends that we admit our humanness and draw the pattern for our lives around His divineness. It is not unspiritual to make mistakes. It is only unspiritual when we refuse to admit them.

Another reason we may cling to our fairy-tale existence is that we assume if we are going to have an impact upon lives, we must be someone others can admire and look up to. The problem is that when we always have to look up to someone, we usually get a bad crick in the neck. Looking up also gives us a distorted view of things; people always appear to be bigger when we are looking up.

When our relationships are vertical, we tend to be very aware of who is on the top and who is on the bottom. Respect does not need a ladder arrangement. If awe is what we want people to feel toward us, then we need to keep our ladders. But if warmth and respect and love are the feelings we want to evoke, then we should put away our ladders and be willing to stand on the ground beside people.

When Paul was writing to the young pastor Timothy, he told

Timothy to be an example of what the believer should be in speech, conduct, love, faith, and purity (1 Tim. 4:12). However, in the very same passage Paul says, "Give yourself wholly to them, so that everyone may see your progress" (4:15). Paul did not say, "Be a perfect example, and don't let anyone know you have room for improvement." Paul's advice to Timothy was: Grow, learn, discover, take pains, absorb yourself, and through your process and progress you will influence other lives.

Jesus Himself had some things to say about people who pretended to be something they were not. He called them "whitewashed tombs . . . full of dead men's bones" (Matt. 23:27). His hammer hit hard against pretense and hypocrisy.

One day Joan, a high schooler, rang my doorbell. She was a controlled, thoughtful girl, and her thoughts came forth in an organized fashion. She was having some trouble with her application of Christianity to her life. "I came to you because you always seem bubbly and on top of things. How do you do it?"

I gave her some of my pat formulas for bubbliness, prayed with her, and she left. During the next three years of Joan's high school experience, I watched her from a distance. Whenever I asked, things were always going fine, and we talked superficially about "on top" things. Joan disappeared into college.

One day several years later, Joan came home from college and sat in on a series I was teaching for a Sunday School class. It was a series that had grown from a personal dilemma I had studied and agonized through. It was a series that didn't give the solutions all tied up in a neat little package, but it did raise some questions about Scripture's implications for living.

Joan came to visit me again after that Sunday School class. In fact she came to visit me quite often after that. We drank many cups of coffee together, thought together, discussed together, disagreed together, prayed together, and grew together. My pat formulas did not bring Joan and me together. My vulnerability did. Our respect for each other did not come while I handed down solutions; it came as we sat across the table from one another and were people involved in a process.

Another reason we may work hard to keep up the fairy-tale

myth of "all's well on the Christian front" is that we fear rejection. We are not sure how people will feel about us if they know we get angry and yell at our kids sometimes. We're not sure how they will respond to our saying, "I'm sorry. I was wrong about that." Or, "I shouldn't have done that." And so we tiptoe on eggshells and get sore feet, because walking on eggshells is not very comfortable. And if we're not comfortable with ourselves there is a good chance others are not comfortable with us either.

When we live under fear of rejection, the safest place for us is in a shell. The trouble with a shell is that it keeps us from people. If we want to touch people, we have to get out of our shell and take some risks. People will not always understand. Sometimes they will criticize or jump to wrong conclusions. But in the process of our own growth, we may unearth a response in others which may have been buried deep within their own facade.

Our honesty can hurt when it hits so close to another's shell, but it can force them to come out and take a long, hard look at themselves. However, in our honesty with others we may find common denominators which allow us to solve the problem together; we may evoke feelings that need to surface. And then God can give us the gentle touch of healing.

One day I shared with some friends some of my fears about death. I told them about lying in bed at night and visualizing a cold, sterile operating room and a surgeon who was about to embark on an exploration for cancer in my body. Cancer is part of my family history, and every woman I heard about who died of cancer would become me.

Even as I talked with friends about it, I was learning to face my fears. Others jumped into the conversation, and what followed was a healthy and honest appraisal of death and our feelings about it. Only Jill remained quiet. I did not know her well, but I could tell it was a difficult discussion for her to hear.

Not long after this discussion, I was in Jill's home for lunch. "Your conversation about death the other week was very hard for me." She initiated the subject. "But it was also good for me. I buried my nineteen-month-old three years ago, and I buried my feelings with her." As she cried, I watched three years of pent-up emotions and silent grief come pouring out.

Now I don't know whether Christians are supposed to go around telling people that they are afraid to die. Perhaps we are to encourage others by talking about the blessed hope. I believe in that blessed hope with all my heart. I know that when the time comes to accept the fact of death, the resources of God will be at my disposal. I also know that God's resources are available for any Christian who goes through death. But I will not pretend to others that my fears do not exist here and now.

Sometimes all is not well in my house. Sometimes all is not well with me. Allowing myself the freedom to say that is allowing myself the freedom to be a person who lives life with both feet firmly on the ground. And the ground is a whole lot safer than a pedestal or an ivory tower.

Nevertheless, some may say, "it is not healthy to bare your soul with everyone. Too much honesty may strip away those private sectors that house the soul—the place where hopes, dreams, fears, disappointments, and tears rest sheltered from the probing view of the public. True there are parts of me I don't want to and don't need to share with everyone. To do so would not only cheapen me but would cheapen the gift I give to others. There will always be, and indeed, must always be, space in my life for privacy. Parts of me I will give gladly and publicly—my time, my abilities, my skills and my expertise. Parts of me I will give selectively to those closest to me—my hopes, my fears, my joys, my tears. But there is still a third part—the private core which may be so cherished I share it with no one.

Admitting my humanness does not mean I violate my need to store in secret some of the treasures of my heart. I find an example in Mary who, after the shepherds had viewed the Christ Child of Bethlehem, "treasured up all these things and pondered these things in her heart. . . . " (Luke 2:19). We do not need to feel pressured to tell all, nor should we feel guilty when we do not. However, when it comes to allowing people to identify with us, to see that we are pilgrims in progress, there is perhaps nothing more important than candor.

Even candor has its limits though. I must always take into consideration the comfort level of those who are recipients of my honesty. If my transparency makes others feel they are looking into windows which should be closed and shuttered, or if others feel I have violated my own space with them—forced them to come too close when they should have remained farther off, then perhaps I have bared too much. Others may not always be able to verbalize their discomfort with my honesty, but awkward silences, hasty changes of subject, sudden loss of eye contact may send the message. Candor must always be coupled with discretion and appropriateness.

Why is it important to appropriately admit to humanness? For another's sake yes. But also for my sake. I need to give myself permission to be a pilgrim in process. Even as I admit to earthly deprivations and fluctuations I am learning anew to appreciate grace and to bask in the glory of unconditional, Heavenly Father love. I am also learning accountability for the next time around.

Interaction Time
Personal Reflection
1. If others had to categorize me as distant and aloof or warm and approachable, I think they would say. . . .

2. I . . .
_____ readily admit my humanness to others.
_____ occasionally admit my humanness to others.
_____ seldom admit my humanness to others.
_____ never admit my humanness to others.

3. As near as I can tell, the reason for my above answer is. . . .

4. A time when I was transparent with another and the results were positive was. . . .

5. A time when I was transparent with another and the results were less than positive was. . . .

6. I coped with that situation by. . . .

7. I have not yet recovered from that situation but am working on it by. . . .

8. I basically feel others are (comfortable, uncomfortable) with my openness.

9. If others are uncomfortable with my openness one thing I might do differently is. . . .

10. I am basically (at peace, dissatisfied) with the level of transparency I have with others.

11. If I were asking for Heavenly Father help in the area of transparency I would say. . . .

Group Interaction

1. How much of our humanity do you think others need to see?

2. Do you agree or disagree with the following statement: Christian leaders, of all people, should be willing to admit their humanness? Why?

3. What observations have you made over your years as a pastor's wife about transparency in relationships with the people of your congregation?

4. When has it worked for you?

5. When has it worked against you?

6. How do you know when it is time, if ever, to be candid with the people of your church?

7. How do you know when it is *not* time?

8. How do you keep transparency from becoming fuel for

gossip or opportunity for parishioners to merely satisfy their curiosity about their pastor's wife?

9. What principles from scripture apply to the issue of admitting humanness?

10. What principles support the side of limited restraint when it comes to admitting humanness? For example, how might the principle of restrained freedom in 1 Corinthians 7 apply to the issue? What other principles can you think of?

11. Do you feel it is important to God that we learn to admit our humanness? Why or why not?

12. What is the most important lesson you have learned as a pastor's wife about transparency?

FIVE

What's a Nice Person Like You Doing with a Feeling Like That? *Learning to Acknowledge and Deal with Feelings*

The days were long and hot. The nights were short and hot. The perimeters of my physical world had expanded to Mexico, but the boundaries of my domestic world had shrunk to a path between kitchen, marketplace, and bed. My kitchen-market-bed routine took my total concentration. What would have been a normal, three-minute, over-the-counter meat purchase back home became a thirty-minute ordeal of staring a pig in the face while I tried to decide which of his sides I wanted for dinner. Once my decision was made, I had to make the man who tended hanging pigs understand what I wanted.

What happened to that pig between the market stall and the dinner plate is a plot for a suspense novel. What does one do with a piece of raw meat fresh off the pig when there is a pot, one small burner, water that is unsafe to drink, one box of Morton's salt, and twenty mouths to feed? It was my job to find out, so I did. Others dug ditches, hammered nails, scraped, painted, and cleaned. I peeled, chopped, grated, diced, boiled, fried, and baked.

My dedication to my job left little time for extracurricular activities. Mark blended in with the other nineteen mouths that needed to be fed. Somewhere between midnight and dawn, I would manage an exhausted little "good night" as I dropped into my sleeping bag beside him. He grunted his acknowledgment, and the day ended.

By night twenty-one, my silent partner could be silent no longer. "I don't feel like you belong to me any more. I'm tired of sharing you with everyone else. I'm glad we're going home."

I could not believe what I was hearing from my strong, confident, self-assured, independent husband. "Now you know how I've felt sometimes during the past seven years," was my only response, and the conversation ended.

But it was not forgotten. Back home in the air-conditioned comfort of a restaurant, our discussion was continued. I had cracked open the door to some of my pent-up emotions about Mark's job. I could no longer worry that Mark would reject my feelings or misunderstand them or think me unspiritual because of them. I could no longer pretend those emotions were not there. And so I took a deep breath and said, "Sometimes I have felt neglected. Sometimes I have felt that you are married to the church. Sometimes I have felt that you do not belong to me." The door had been opened. At least now we could both take a long, hard look at what was inside.

Why it took me seven years to share my honest feelings with Mark I'm not sure. I suppose down deep I may have felt that if I ignored them long enough they would go away. The problem was that they didn't go away. In fact, they usually intensified.

If I began to think of Mark as a house guest because he was gone so much one week, the next week I would view him as a total stranger. When the lid blew off, it would be for something as minor as his leaving his jogging clothes all over the bedroom floor because he had to hurry off to a meeting. It was much easier to blame the problem on messy habits than to deal with feelings of neglect. The original hurt was not doctored; we were just applying Band-Aids. But Band-Aids don't cure infections.

My reluctance to share my feelings with Mark was complicated by the fact that I segregated my feelings into good and bad. There was no question in my mind that it was not a good thing for a pastor's wife to resent her husband's job. In fact, it was a selfish response. My selfishness, I concluded, was due to my lack of spiritual maturity. I became my own judge and pronounced myself guilty with a capital G. Now I not only had my resentment, my selfishness, my lack of spiritual maturity to deal with, but I also had a giant case of guilt on my hands. If you don't think that is a complicated maze to work through, just try it sometime. Judging myself and feeling guilty did not help me deal with my feelings any more realistically than putting Band-Aids on them had.

Another reason I kept the door so tightly closed on my feelings was my rugged individualism: If it's my problem, I'll slug it out alone. I've always been one to accept personal challenges. If there is a mountain to be climbed, I will climb it just to prove I can do it. If there is a cave to be explored, I will crawl on my tummy in the dark for five hours just to say I can do it, even though I panic in an elevator. I have observed, however, that rugged individualism can sometimes be too individual and personal challenges can sometimes be too personal.

Assuming that it's just my problem is one sure way to further isolate myself from Mark. By determining to slug it out alone, I am compounding my aloneness. I am saying to him, "I'll share with you the things that I feel I'm handling correctly, but if I feel I'm blowing it I'll never tell." That leaves out a pretty significant portion of my life.

That also leaves Mark stumbling around in the dark trying to guess what it is that's bothering me, because I communicate my feelings to him whether I say them or not. When I am unwilling to verbally pinpoint them for him, he is left with no alternative but to play a guessing game about my nonverbal clues. Is it a headache? Naughty kids? The weather? The time of month? The time of year? What I'm wearing? My breath? The neighbors? Her book? His choices are endless.

If Mark loses at his wife-reading game, he is in double trouble. It goes like this: Mark comes home from work. He sees my tight lips and narrow eyes. I don't volunteer any information. His detective work begins. He surveys the evidence and decides the children have been extra naughty today, so he tries hard to lighten my load with them. But he's missed his clue. My tight lips and narrow eyes are really saying, "I'm upset with you because you didn't schedule me in for a lunch with you this week."

Now not only is he in trouble because he didn't take me out for lunch, but he is also in trouble because he has not been sensitive to what my narrow eyes and tight lips are telling him.

Rugged individualism may get me over the mountains and through the caves, but it will not get me through the interpersonal tensions of life. No problem is ever just my own. Somewhere, somehow, someone will be affected.

The opposite extreme of the it's-just-my-hang-up-and-I'll-slug-it-out-alone-method of dealing with emotions is the it's-all-his-hang-up-he-made-me-do-it-method. I may have a good case in my favor. I may have every reason in the book to feel slighted because Mark didn't take me out for lunch, but Mark did not make me feel resentful. I allowed myself to feel resentful. By placing the blame for my feelings on someone else, in this case Mark, I do not have to assume responsibility for my own actions and attitudes.

When I blame Mark for my resentment, it does not take him long to catch on. I use the pronoun "you" quite often. I don't take a breath between my sentences—that way he doesn't have a chance to interrupt. I also avoid eye or any other kind of contact. When Mark receives that kind of treatment, I've issued an open invitation for defensiveness. And when the defense is launched, we're in a battle, not a discussion. There is all the difference in the world in telling Mark how I feel and telling him how he's made me feel.

There have also been times when I have used the pressure cooker approach to handling my emotions. Generally, I do not plan to use that approach. But if I do not open my safety valve from time to time, the pressure cooker phenomenon will occur. Explosions are a quick way to let it all out, but explosions generally take a long time to clean up.

I remember my mother-in-law telling me about the day she cooked beans in her pressure cooker to feed some unexpected company. She needed a quick method but forgot one minor precaution, and spent the rest of the day scraping beans off her kitchen ceiling.

I have discovered that it is not only important *how* I report my feelings, but it is important when I report my feelings.

It was retreat season again. After two weekends at home alone with the children, I was looking forward to once more including weekends in our social calendar. With such joyful thoughts in mind, I welcomed one very exhausted youth director in out of the ice and snow at 1:00 A.M.

"Aren't you glad retreats are over for this year?" I asked as we thawed out his feet which had frozen because the heater on the van was broken.

"Well, they are not exactly over yet. Mike is short on staff for next week. I said I'd go to help him out."

Now I have nothing against junior high retreats except when they are scheduled for the night that we had planned to celebrate some friends' anniversary with them. I gently reminded the frozen youth director of his previous commitment.

At 1:00 A.M. following a three-day retreat, the frozen youth director had one thought on his mind—sleep. I reluctantly followed him to bed and smoldered under the covers. After about the sixth solid snore from him, I could take his unresponsiveness no longer. I had feelings that needed to be reported. It wasn't fair that he could sleep and I couldn't. With grim determination to be transparent in this marriage, I sat straight up in bed (in such a way that would waken any slumbering, semi-frozen youth director), turned on the light, and proceeded to report my feelings.

Mark had no choice. He sat up, propped his drooping eyelids open, and listened. Having to cancel an anniversary celebration for a junior high retreat wasn't the only thing I had on my mind. In fact, the more I talked the more I had on my mind. The more I had on my mind the more upset I got. At 1:30 A.M. it is very easy to find lots of things to be upset about, especially when your husband has been gone for three days.

"Now may I tell you how I feel," Mark asked calmly after I had reported feelings I hadn't even known I had until I started my report session. "I feel tired. Could we table this discussion until morning?"

It was amazing the difference that a sunny morning, a cup of hot tea, and a good night of sleep made on that conversation. Our marriage was not in nearly as bad shape as it had been just the night before. Mark did not double schedule commitments nearly as often as it had seemed he did when I thought about it at 1:30 A.M. I was even able to remember the main point of our discussion—what to do about a junior high retreat and an anniversary celebration which were scheduled for the same night.

It didn't take us long to work out a compromise. Camp Timberlee was only two hours away, and Mark could easily slip away for the dinner celebration with friends and still be back at camp before he was needed again. How could we have overlooked such an obvious solution?

I'm not sure why that 1:30 A.M. session took place. It may have been my way of hurting the person whom I felt had caused my discomfort. Maybe it was my way of getting the attention I felt I had been deprived of for three days. Or perhaps I felt that listening to myself talk was better than staring into a dark room and listening to someone snore. Looking back over that scene, I have serious questions as to the how, the when, and the why of that report. But at least there was an attempt. The delicate skill required in verbalizing feelings comes with experience.

Another helpful way to handle my feelings has been trying to anticipate them. When I do this, I can make provision for them.

One of my favorite overnight spots in Chicago is Oakbrook's Hyatt Regency hotel. It was the very spot that the church staff and board decided on for their annual retreat—without wives. I dreamed wistfully about a weekend at the Hyatt Regency. Along about Wednesday I began to dread the weekend of sit-

ting home alone with the children. I anticipated that my feelings of gloom would not get any lighter as the weekend came
closer.

About the next best thing to going to the Hyatt Regency is
going to the farm of some very dear friends. And since it was
time to compensate for my feelings, I picked up the phone and
invited myself. Our friends were delighted; so were the children
and I. The weekend was a big success.

Now, I could have sat home and been a martyr about it all,
or felt resentful that wives weren't included in the retreat.
Another alternative would have been to count all the times
Mark got to eat steak while I ate soup with the kids, or to call
my mother and remind her to keep praying because being a
pastor's wife involves so many sacrifices. But I enjoy the farm
much more than I enjoy sitting around being a martyr. Also,
I'm a much more pleasant person to be with when I'm not
being a martyr. Therefore, for all involved, the trip to the farm
was a much better alternative.

Expressing and anticipating my emotions have provided helpful insights, but they have not been the whole lesson. I have
learned that from God's point of view I am responsible to learn
control of those emotions which are so much a part of being
human. I am not to be a victim of them. God has given me the
gift of self-control to take care of that (Gal. 5:22-23). My
emotions do not need to color my view of the whole world or
paralyze me and keep me from doing what needs to be done.
Emotions need not be the control tower for my actions or the
roller-coaster ride that pulls me through life.

I don't believe God intends that I boycott my emotions or
that I become a stoic. Life will have its emotional highs and
lows. What self-control means is that God has given me resources to handle my emotions in a godly way.

One of the things self-control enables me to do is to keep
things in perspective. My emotions can easily distort my view
of reality. I can draw conclusions on the basis of how I feel or
make decisions from an emotional rather than from a rational
point of view.

Peter describes the results of self-control: "For if you possess these qualities (including self-control, 2 Peter 1:6) in increasing measure, they will keep you from being ineffective and unproductive in your knowledge of our Lord Jesus Christ. But if anyone does not have them, he is nearsighted and blind" (2 Peter 1:8-9).

If I operate my life on the feeling level, there are often days when I would have to conclude that God is not love because I don't always have that warm-fuzzy-loved feeling. I may feel neglected by God. And while the feeling is valid, I must recognize it as a feeling, not a fact. God has not neglected me even though it appears that way to me at the moment. Scripture tells me that God is love, and this fact doesn't depend on whether I feel it or not. God's love for me is a fact, not a feeling.

Failure to recognize how my emotions are affecting me can lead me to wrong conclusions.

One thing that smashed my pastor's-wife fantasy was that business hours for the pastor are often night hours. When the honeymoon ended, I found myself with many empty evenings, and I began to feel ignored and neglected. I tried various approaches toward my empty-evening disappointment. I offered my assistance in rearranging the youth pastor's schedule for him. I gave repeat performances about why a wife needs her husband home in the evenings after being away from him all day. I kept score; nights away versus nights home. Nights away always won. I became a martyr. I saved all my work for the evening so I'd have plenty to keep my mind occupied. As a result, evenings became drudgery. I went to bed early to forget, but the empty side of the bed wouldn't let me.

The twilight hours were fast dimming the glow of our marriage. The number of evenings out was becoming the gauge for how much Mark did or did not love me. He must be planning committee meetings just so he would have somewhere to spend his evenings. I was totally immersed in self-pity.

Fortunately, the illogic of my logic soon caught up with me, and I realized that I was reacting emotionally. It might be possible that evenings out were as hard on Mark as they were on me. My emotions had blinded me to that possibility. My view of how things really were had been distorted by how I felt.

I decided some things had to change. First, I decided that when Mark said he loved me, he meant it. His evenings away from home had nothing whatsoever to do with the degree of his love for me. That there would be evenings alone was simply a fact of my life. Secondly, I decided to change my agenda for evenings. Instead of washing my kitchen floor, ironing, or baking, I put on soft music, built a fire in the fireplace, and sat down with a good book. I also stopped going to bed alone.

My attitude toward evening has slowly changed, although my situation has stayed the same. Mark is still gone most evenings. But after-dinner hours have become my favorite time of the day. I save them for the things I like to do the most and look forward to their peace and privacy.

Peter suggests that self-control is directly related to our effectiveness and productivity as servants of God (2 Peter 1:8). To deny my feelings is to deny myself. To know how to control those feelings means effective, productive living.

Given then, that feelings are neither good nor bad, feelings simply are. It is the amount of control I choose to exercise over those feelings that renders them either good or bad. God's provision is for me to control rather than be controlled by the emotive side of my person. How then do I know which of the two tendencies—to control or to be controlled by my emotions—is true in my life?

Mismanaged emotions always show up in relationships. Evidence that my emotions may need tighter reign may include: others have to tiptoe around me, or cannot speak their feelings or their mind for fear it will trigger disruption of relationship between us—pouting, moodiness, verbal outbursts, prolonged silence; with every slight mood change the way I treat my family changes; innocent people are affected by my feelings which may have originally been directed toward someone else; I go from emotional highs to emotional lows in a very short period of time; on the other hand, getting over anger, disappointment, misunderstanding, hurt, takes a great deal of time; I am always feeling hurt about something or another.

Monitoring and supervising my emotions is no simple task. It calls for help from the One who delights in doing for me what I cannot do for myself. It also may call for help from a spouse, a trusted friend, or a trained counselor who may spot and call to my attention the games I allow my emotions to play with me. Admitting the power of my emotions and analyzing the effects they are having on me and on my relationships may well be the first steps toward learning to handle my emotions in ways that bring freedom and peace to daily living.

Interaction Time
Personal reflection:
1. The part of this chapter I most closely identified with was. . . .

2. When I am upset my usual method for handling my emotions is. . . .

3. The way this affects my husband is. . . .

4. The way this affects my children is. . . .

5. I think the way I handle my emotional highs and lows is (healthy, unhealthy) because. . . .

6. I felt I handled an emotional low correctly when. . . .

7. What I did in that situation was. . . .

8. What I learned through that situation was. . . .

9. A time when I felt I handled an emotional low incorrectly was. . . .

10. What I did in that situation was. . . .

11. What I learned through that situation was. . . .

12. When it comes to handling my emotions, I feel I am (too controlled, not controlled enough).

13. One thing about handling my emotions that I would like to do differently is. . . .

14. One step I might take in that direction is. . . .

15. My prayer toward that end is. . . .

Group Interaction
1. Do you think pastor's wives in general, feel more guilty than others when they have emotional lows? Why or why not?

2. Can people be too controlled with their emotions?

3. If so, what are the negative consequences?

4. What are some danger signs that emotions are not controlled enough? What might be done if this is the case?

5. Is there ever a time when reporting feelings can do more harm than good? When?

6. If there is a time when reporting feelings can do more harm than good, what might people do instead with their feelings?

7. What have you done with feelings that had potential for negative consequence, especially when those feelings were directed toward your husband or his ministry?

8. What was the end result?

9. What was the lesson learned?

10. What advice would you give to a pastor's wife who is struggling with emotions that have disruptive potential?

11. What principle or passage from Scripture has been or might be particularly helpful in the handling of your emotions?

S I X

Private Property: Keep Out!
Learning to Work through Resentment

What do you do when the phone rings at two in the morning? You sit straight up in bed and panic over which one of your relatives has died. At least that's what I did. I was relieved to hear Mark say, "Keep him there. I'll be right over." However my relief was soon to give way to a much less generous response. After all, it was two o'clock Monday morning. Sundays were not exactly days of rest at our house. Of all the nights we needed sleep, it was Sunday night.

That particular early Monday morning hour was complicated by the fact that we had entertained a houseful of company after church on Sunday night. Another reason we shouldn't be disturbed was that I was eight months, one week, and three days

pregnant. Sleep just didn't come easily to one in such a condi-
tion. And when it did come, I wasn't any too willing to see it
go.

"Tom has overdosed again. He's hallucinating. I'll probably
bring him here until he comes around." And with that Mark
was down the stairs and out the door. The fact that it truly was
an emergency did not seem to make things any easier. It never
occurred to me that drug overdoses don't wait for daylight or for
the youth pastor to get his eight hours of sleep.

What seemed to matter more was that I was about to have a
baby, needed my sleep, and needed my husband. Tom had
family. Couldn't they assume responsibility for him at least
until office hours? Why did it always have to be Mark they
called? Probably what Tom needed right now was a doctor more
than a pastor. Mark had often gone beyond his call of duty for
Tom, and that was OK as long as the call didn't come in the
middle of the night.

When I had sufficiently stewed over the fact that my husband was taken from me at two in the morning to make a
pastoral call, I moved on to other things. For instance, Mark
was bringing Tom here to my house. Now, I knew enough
about drug addicts to be certain that there was potential vio-
lence in someone who was hallucinating from a bad trip. I
envisioned my newly painted, white, colonial front door with a
hole through it and my fragile, antique, Queen Anne's chair
being smashed to pieces. What was worse, I pictured my husband with a black eye or a crushed jaw. Tom was no little
person to fool with.

With such positive thoughts in mind, I waited for the return
of the wild. I heard the front door open gently, the muffled
voices of people talking, the quiet tread of feet going downstairs
to the family room.

When an hour had passed with no loud outbursts, I decided
I'd been a little unfair. The next thing I remembered was Mark
leaning over me and whispering that Tom had agreed to go to
the psychiatric ward over at the hospital. I heard my freshly
painted, white, colonial front door, which was still in one
piece, close quietly. They had gone.

The story of Tom's hallucinations didn't end there. This time Tom had done himself up right. It took him days to get over his demonic, middle-of-the-night dreams. And when his dreams hit, his call came—sometimes two, three, or four o'clock in the morning. With each middle-of-the-night crisis, I found myself a little less resentful. I began to think less in terms of Mark as my husband and more of him as Tom's companion in crisis. I stopped thinking about myself and acting as though I owned Mark Senter. Tom needed him during those hellish hours far more than I did. Where Mark belonged was with Tom. By the end of the week, I was literally crying for a person so controlled by the powers of darkness.

Why the initial resentment of Tom's intrusion into our night sleep? I think it had something to do with the use of the little word "my." It was *my* husband who had to be shared. It was *my* valuable sleep that was being interrupted. It was *my* house that was being invaded. *My* is possessive. When it is used as an adjective, it is harmless. But when my becomes an attitude, I'm headed for trouble. I am posting my life with "Private Property: Keep Out" signs.

The problem with possessiveness is that it usually leads to resentment. If I feel strongly about the ownership of my yard, I will resent the fact that you cut through my yard on your way to a friend's house. If I feel strongly about the ownership of my time, I will resent the fact that the phone keeps interrupting. If I have the strings tied securely to my husband, I will resent the fact that other people will need him and that their needs are not always during convenient hours.

One of the most important lessons I have learned is that I do not own my husband. The marriage certificate is not a deed to property. If I feel that I own him, I become possessive. If I feel that the church owns him, I become resentful. Therefore, the safest and happiest way is to let the Lord and Mark have joint ownership over Mark.

There is a big difference between feeling that my husband belongs to me and feeling that he is a part of me. Ownership is likely to leave the door wide open for resentment when others need my husband. Partnership is sharing something of myself when I share my husband with others.

A possessive attitude is fertile soil for resentment. But resentment may also stem from the feeling that life owes me certain benefits. It is easy to assume that we deserve some special treatment just because of who we are or what we've done or whose wife we happen to be.

For example, the pastor's wife—certainly the church owes her some consideration. Look at all she does for them. She deserves remembrances at Christmas. Think of all the sacrifices she has made for the congregation during the year. She should sit at the head table for the annual spring women's luncheon. Look at all the times she takes a back seat to her up-front husband. And a Sunday dinner now and then on someone else's charge card doesn't hurt the pastor's family either. Everyone knows how hard Sundays are on the pastor's wife.

Now I'm not opposed to Christmas gifts for the pastor, pastor's wives sitting at the head tables, or inviting the pastor's family out for Sunday dinner. But I am opposed to the attitude that says, "I deserve this because of whose wife I am or because of what I've done for you." Such an attitude is bound to lead to resentment when all the benefits don't come flying in.

Jesus had plenty of reason to feel resentful for the treatment, or lack thereof that He received from other people. After all, He was the Son of God. He could have gently reminded people of that fact when they seemed to be overlooking Him. He could have pulled out His identification card and flaunted it in the face of those who were not giving Him proper respect.

But He didn't. Instead, He chose to humble Himself and become a servant (Phil. 2:6-7). He was not concerned with what the world owed Him because He was the Son of God, but what He owed the world because He was the Son of God. He reminded His disciples more than once that He had come not to be served, but to serve (Mark 10:45; Luke 22:27).

A true servant has no expectations of what he will get or what he deserves. True giving is not centered on self but on others. It does not think in terms of the round-trip benefits. However, the interesting thing is that as we give, we do in fact receive. Jesus said, "Give, and it will be given to you" (Luke

6:38). This is not a reason for giving, but the result of giving.

Living with the attitude that God and others owe us special favors because of all we've done is one quick way to end up with a heart full of bitterness and resentment. I know. I learned the hard way.

It happened at a church where the pastor still lived in the church's parsonage. In fact, our church owned two parsonages—a large, spacious, two-story colonial and a smaller, two-bedroom ranch. It was perfectly logical that the senior pastor who had three children should live in the large colonial and the youth pastor who had one child should live in the smaller ranch.

This was a happy arrangement until the senior pastor bought his own home and moved out of the parsonage and the church board decided to sell the three-bedroom colonial. The "For Sale" sign went up, and weeds began to grow. No one was interested in buying, so that luscious, three-bedroom colonial sat empty.

Meanwhile, just down the block, I looked longingly toward the colonial. I made daily trips down the street on my bike to see if there was a "Sold" sign yet. As the months passed and the weeds continued to grow, our own little ranch seemed to be getting smaller and smaller. It had only two bedrooms, and our second child was on the way. Surely the church board couldn't miss the fact that I was pregnant. Surely they knew our house had just two bedrooms.

I needed that house. I deserved that house. After all, they expected me to be hostess for high school kids who packed out every inch of our tiny ranch, including the bathroom. They expected us to have committee meetings in a living room that held about six chairs if you sat in front of the fireplace. And all the while that large home sat empty just down the block.

It didn't matter that the church needed the money from the parsonage sale for investment elsewhere. It didn't matter that building upkeep is costly and time-consuming. What mattered to poor, neglected me was that someone was not sensitive to my needs.

The sad thing was that I not only resented the fact that I was not invited to move into the parsonage when I had fully expected the invitation and the fact that the board had made the decision to sell the property, but I also began to resent people. I resented their large homes with two-car garages, their boats, their swimming pools, their airplanes, their snowmobiles, their horses, their trips, their clothes, their on-the-town dining. So I sat in my little two-bedroom ranch and shook my head that God's people could be so calloused.

And then one day I woke up and found to my horror that I was walling myself in—cut off by my own resentment. I was no longer enjoying people of the church as I had before. I began to feel uncomfortable and discontent with them. I began to criticize and compare. The very people I had genuinely loved so much were fast becoming strangers at the expense of my growing resentment.

The realization was rather sudden: No house was more important than my relationships with people. No third bedroom was more important than loving the body to which I belonged. I knew, something had to change.

I began to look around for things I liked about our little house. One definite advantage was that the smallness kept housecleaning chores to a minimum. I had always loved the two big blue spruce trees that provided the background from our living room windows. I remembered that I had always wanted a window above the kitchen sink that faced the street so I could watch the world move outside. We had a perfect front-yard view from the window above our kitchen sink.

Gradually, I stopped visiting the "For Sale" sign, and I stopped dreaming about how I would decorate the nursery. I began to forget who had the boats and horses and spacious houses. It simply did not matter any more.

And then one spring evening the chairman of the church board phoned. They were taking down the "For Sale" sign and moving in a painting crew. The house would be ours within the month. The board wives hung the wallpaper, cleaned the windows, scrubbed the floors. They brought in hot meals, took care of Jori, and even planted flowers in the yard. A member of the board offered his moving van complete with personnel. And then to celebrate the happy event, board members threw a giant, housewarming surprise party.

No one has ever enjoyed a house more than I enjoyed that parsonage. And I'm convinced one of the reasons I enjoyed it so much was that I stopped struggling so hard to attain it. When it came, it was a happy, unexpected bonus and not something the church owed me because of all I had done for it.

Resentment grows, not only from a possessive spirit and an I-deserve-this attitude, it also finds root in our need to control. As long as our plans are enforced, our schedules intact, our children appropriate and acceptable, our husbands attentive and cooperative, we are peaceful, lovely and amiable. But let our neat little systems be thwarted by any one of the myriads of life's disrupters and resentment sets in. We may resent ourselves at our own inability to keep our world in orbit, but more than likely our resentment will direct itself toward the event, organization or person who has been the disrupter—the church, our husband's schedule, our children's undependability, the church board's policies.

When resentment stems from the thwarting of our need to control, the natural tendency is to come on stronger. We try harder to manipulate the world around us—our husband's schedule, our children's actions, the church board's policy. We become involved where we should have stayed uninvolved. We seek out information we should have left unsought. We talk when we should remain silent. We rearrange when we should let well enough alone. We seek to alter where there is no need for altering. All may be done with the air of involvement, but underneath, it may be the fires of resentment that move us—resentment that we are not in charge, that someone or something else calls the shots and determines our days.

Interestingly enough, for those of us who believe that ultimately God is in control of our days, that He proposes and disposes, acquiescing to God's plan for our life is usually much more acceptable to us than acquiescing to other's plans for our lives. We do not protest nearly so loudly when God brings those things into our lives over which we have no control, such as illnesses or natural infirmities, as we do when others bring into our lives those things over which we have no control—salaries, bonuses, schedules, policies, vacation days, etc. But if we are ever to rid ourselves of resentment, the two—God's control over us and human controls over us, must be viewed as one. Yes, God proposes and disposes but He usually does so through the people He places over us. There is seldom an individual who is not subject to some human control of one sort or another. Submitting ourselves to another's control is perhaps the hardest reality of ministry, and probably the greatest source of personal heartache and corporate pain. We do not own our husbands. Yes. But also, we do not own ourselves or our time. The sooner we as pastors' wives admit to the fact, the less likelihood that resentment will find a permanent home in our hearts.

Resentment, like all emotions, is not self-contained. What is in our heart will surely show up on our face. It is hard to keep resentment a secret. Therefore, it seems the choice is clear. We can become a picture of hardness—face set with resentment written in every wrinkle, or we can choose to let the lines of contentment calm and mellow us so that those who look into our face see God's peace which comes from a lifetime of accepting that which we cannot control.

"Godliness with contentment is great gain," the Apostle Paul says (1 Tim. 6:6). He wrote those words during the short years between his two imprisonments when he was living under a death threat from Nero, the most powerful man in the world. Paul had every reason in the world to dismiss the word "contentment" from his vocabulary, but he had "learned to be content whatever the circumstances" (Phil. 4:11).

When contentment becomes a way of life, there is no room for resentment and bitterness.

Interaction Time
Personal Reflection

1. If someone asked me for a definition of resentment, I would answer. . . .

2. If I had to name potential causes of resentment in my life, I would say. . . .

3. I struggled with the issue of resentment when. . . .

4. Resentment is usually attached to a person or persons. When I felt resentment toward someone, I dealt with the person or persons by. . . .

5. The result was. . . .

6. In looking back, what I learned from the situation was. . . .

7. Which of the two describe me:
___ I have occasional moments of resentment.
___ I am a resentful person.
A step I need to take in dealing with my moments of resentment is. . . .
A step I need to take toward finding out why I am a resentful person is. . . .

8. I (do, do not) feel that I generally know the root(s) of my resentment.

9. I (do, do not) feel that I generally know what to do about my resentment and (can, cannot) bring a certain degree of resolution.

10. Read through the book of Philippians.
What reasons did Paul have for resentment?
What clues do you have that he did not choose resentment?
What attitudes did he possess that kept him from becoming resentful?

11. Write a prayer telling God what you need from Him in your struggle against resentment.

Group Interaction
1. What observations could you make about a person who is resentful?

2. Name some attitudes which often lead to resentment.

3. One of the unique challenges for the ministry wife is sharing her husband with many others. How have you been able to keep this fact of life from becoming a root of resentment? How have you been able to work out from under the load when it has become a root of resentment?

4. What has helped you to keep from becoming resentful when you felt a church board or another staff member was being unfair to you?

5. There are no doubt, people in your congregation who earn much higher salaries than your husband's. What keeps you content? How do you work through the times when you're not content?

6. Do you agree with the statement: "Don't expect anything from anyone and then you're never disappointed." Why or why not?

7. What do you think expectations have to do with resentment?

8. Tell of a time when someone in your congregation did something nice for you that you didn't expect. What was your response? Tell of a time when someone in your congregation didn't do something for you that you did expect them to do. What was your response? What response do you recommend and why?

9. Jesus was in public ministry. He had plenty of reasons to be resentful toward the events and people of His life. What, from the following situations in His life, gives you examples to follow:
- when others let Him down: Matthew 26
- when His authority was questioned: Matthew 21:23-27; 22:15-22

- when He was misunderstood: Matthew 26:6-13
- when He was betrayed: Matthew 26:14-75
- when He was misrepresented: Matthew 26:57-67

10. What would you say if another pastor's wife who was struggling with resentment toward her congregation came to you for advice?

11. What might be the greatest thing you can do to guard yourself against resentment? What might be the greatest thing you can do for another pastor's wife to help her guard herself against resentment? Pray for each other toward that end.

SEVEN

A Husband's World Is Not All Male

Learning to Respond to Other Women in My Husband's Life

There was another woman in my husband's life. She took my place as one of the high school sponsors when I moved on to the business of having a baby, and she appeared to be all that I was not—blond, athletic, skinny, energetic, lively, fun, talented, and dedicated 100 percent to teenagers. I'm brunette, moderately athletic, and at the time I felt neither skinny, energetic, lively, talented, attractive, fun, nor 100 percent dedicated to teenagers. Instead, I found myself on a couch with a pillow against my back and my feet propped up, reading Doctor Spock and *Baby Talk* magazine, knitting a baby blanket, and eating cottage cheese and yogurt.

Meanwhile, as youth pastor, Mark continued to move in a

world of teens and skinny, energetic, attractive, lively, fun, talented, and 100-percent-dedicated-to-teenagers type sponsors.

It was a difficult time for me. I had always been the drama and speech coach for the youth group. Now *she* was the drama and speech coach—a logical move since she taught drama and speech at the high school. I suddenly remembered that I had never taught drama or speech; I was only an amateur. I had always been the one to feed the kids pop and pizza after a Sunday night church service. Suddenly the action switched to *her* place. Everyone went to Sue's. She opened her apartment and let them make their own pizza. Kids came early and stayed late. They discussed their hassles with her and told her their jokes. The niche I had always filled was being filled by another.

The kids spent time with her, and so did Mark. He had to— at sponsors' meetings, Bible studies, teen projects, retreats, parties. Meanwhile, I was sure that Mark was as aware as I was that she was blond, attractive, athletic, skinny, energetic, lively, fun, talented, and 100 percent dedicated to teenagers.

Our baby, Jori, came, and she was soon the youth group's newest project. They watched over her with great care and affection. However, as I became less of a youth sponsor and more of a mother, Sue was gaining in the youth group's popularity polls. It was obvious she was being a great help to Mark too. He needed her talent, aliveness, energy, and dedication. He needed her fresh, new ideas and her sensitive insight into teenagers. He also needed her educational expertise. There was no doubt about it. She was a top-notch youth worker.

Now what I should be saying at this point is that I welcomed my replacement with open arms and warm hospitality. I should be saying that I was grateful for Sue's talent, personality, energy, and dedication; that I thanked God for sending her along to work with Mark in building a strong, solid youth work; that I was happy to see my husband profit from her insights and creativity. I wish I could say that's how it was. But it wasn't. I was too busy comparing myself with her. I was too busy wondering if Mark saw the same things in her that I saw, and maybe more.

I had always felt sorry for wives who weren't secure enough to trust their husbands around other women. I had always felt sorry for wives who didn't consider themselves good enough to hold their husbands' love and watched over them with hawkish eyes and clutching claws. Jealousy, I theorized, would be a sad thing to live with. What was a marriage without trust?

Now, that is a neat little theory as long as things aren't threatening. But real life can become very threatening, and our neat little theories can evaporate under pressure.

But real life can also teach. It can help us refocus, redefine, interpret, and clarify. It has clarified for me over the years that, unless Mark closes himself in a monastery, there will be other women involved in his life. That is simply a fact of life. How I choose to respond to that fact is up to me.

Jealousy is one option, but the writer of Proverbs concluded that "Jealousy rots [life] away" (Prov. 14:30, TLB). Now, if I want to rot away being jealous of all the Sues in life, that's up to me. But I don't get very excited at the prospect. There's nothing attractive about rot.

Conversely, if I get busy and use the resources and situations God has given me, there will be no time for rot to set in.

Suddenly it dawned on me that I could do things at home which I had never had time to do while I was running around being student, youth worker, and employee. I had always wanted to write, and now my opportunity was here. I had almost missed it because I was so busy worrying about someone taking over my territory. As I began redirecting my energies and developing other gifts, Sue gradually became a comfortable part of my life rather than a threat to my happiness.

Mark does not have a "Ruth-sized vacuum" in his heart that only I can fill. He needs other relationships. If I view myself as superwoman, I will try to make myself into all that my husband could ever need, figuring I should be able to fill every corner of his man-sized heart: be his stimulation for sermon topics; his artesian well for new ideas, creative thought, and resource material; his motivation for higher ground; his counselor in times of indecision; his source of strength for weaker moments; and his impetus for fuller development. By the time I'm done with all of that, he shouldn't ever have to glance at another woman. But by then I will have dropped from sheer exhaustion.

I do see myself as an encourager, a motivator, a stimulator, and a resource person for my husband. He is the same for me. But I cannot provide all the stimulation and motivation and resources that Mark needs, just as he cannot do that for me. For me to even think in those terms is absurd. Therefore, it would seem logical that if I can't be Mark's sole provider, he will need other people. And who am I to say which people he can or cannot need? Who am I to censor half of his resource potential simply because of their femaleness?

One of Mark's closest professional associates happens to be a woman. She is an expert in Christian education. She and Mark have developed curriculum, built structures, and been innovative in their field. They are a professional team. I gratefully acknowledge the fact that Diane fills a role in Mark's life that I could never fill. I am not a Christian educator, I do not pretend to be one, and Mark does not try to make me one.

I know what Christian educators do. I listen to their ideas. I read their books now and then. Sometimes I even attend their conventions. But I recognize that Diane is far better equipped than I to provide the expertise and companionship Mark needs in his job as minister of Christian education.

My spot in Mark's life is reserved. Therefore, I don't have to become frantic over the possibility of someone else sitting in my chair. She has her own chair on which to sit. There is room and need for us both in Mark's life.

Mark needs professional relationships. He has social needs that others can fill. But he also has some needs that only I can fill. I must be alert to what I can do for him, but not think I have to do it all. Recognizing the fact that I cannot possibly be everything to Mark has helped me to open the doors to other women in Mark's life in order for his growth to take place.

Another truth I have learned is that not only does Mark need other people, but other people need him and they are not always males.

Cindy was one. In some special way Mark had been able to get through to Cindy when no one else could. She had no father. The only men she knew were the men who came to live with her mother from time to time. Mark had stood by her

through her mother's attempted suicide, had preached the funeral for her mother's boyfriend who was killed in a car acci-
dent, had helped track down her runaway junior high school
brother, and had counseled an older brother who was on drugs.

There were many ways Mark and I were both involved in
Cindy's life. She had lived with us for some time after her
mother's attempted suicide, and she and I had become close.
But when the crises hit, she always called for Mark. He was the
father-big brother image she had never known. In many ways,
he was probably a father image who demonstrated the Heavenly
Father's love to her. There were ways Cindy needed me, but I
also recognized that Mark was providing some intangibles for
her that I could not provide.

Cindy's pregnancy was traumatic for us all. Not many people
knew; she had told us first. She had even volunteered the name
of the father. I assumed her information was accurate, but one
day I heard differently.

Cindy's best friend came to my door one Sunday afternoon
while Mark was away. She came with some information she felt
I should know. According to her source, Mark was the father of
Cindy's baby.

Now what does a wife do with a piece of information like
that? I remember that my voice shook. Whether it was from
shock, anger, amusement, hurt, or grief, I don't know. I man-
aged to remain calm through the rest of the conversation, but
inwardly I felt the walls caving in.

They did cave in. I doubted, I questioned, I was jealous. I
felt insecure. Why did Cindy always need Mark? Why couldn't
she lean on me? What if she were in love with my husband and
he were in love with her?

Mark gently helped me pick up the pieces. He listened to my
feelings and my fears. He took my hurt seriously. He offered me
his love. As we reaffirmed our love and commitment to each
other and to God, the healing began. I asked for an open heart
toward Cindy again. She needed us now more than ever.

The seeds of jealousy and doubt slowly began to wither as I
refused to act upon them. Several months later the source of
the rumor came to Mark, admitted his grievance, and apologized.

There was agony in my experience with Cindy. It hurts even to tell the story. I didn't come through the ordeal with chin up and head held high. But I stood by Cindy even when I realized that the person she needed the most was my husband and not me. Looking back, I realize that jealousy could easily have wiped out our ministry to one very lonely and needy teenage girl. In the end, truth and trust won the case.

Where do my jealousies come from? I've noticed that when I fear rather than trust, I become jealous. Perhaps it is rejection from my husband that I fear. Perhaps I'm afraid that someday I will wake up and find he doesn't love me any more, or has transferred his love to someone else—someone who is prettier, brighter, wittier than I. And so I become suspicious of all women who I consider to have outdone me. Their attractiveness must in some way diminish my own. Because I'm comparing myself with them must mean that Mark is doing the same thing, and in the final count I will lose. In my fear, I stake out the territory for any potential dangers lurking in the dark that could bring about my ultimate rejection. All attractive women are threatening, and I have no alternative but to be jealous.

I may fear because I don't understand the difference between love and sex. The world claims that the two are synonymous—you can't have love without sex. The Bible tells us they are different. Society sings about fleshly, physical love. The Bible speaks of unconditional, giving, agape love. Perhaps my jealousy comes because my view of love has become distorted by the world's view. If I conclude that love is romance and sex, I become suspicious of all love.

What if the pure agape love of one believer for another becomes tarnished by the eros, physical kind of love? The possibility is definitely there. But simply because the possibility is there does not mean that Mark's love and concern for any member of the opposite sex will automatically lead to the bedroom.

Now I'm very much aware of my own humanness. I am also very much aware of the humanness of my husband. I am not naive enough to believe that every second glance Mark gives to a member of the female sex is always done in the name of agape. I am not naive enough to say that I always interpret a hug from a man to be a brother-in-Christ type of hug. It may well depend on who is giving me the hug. I am not naive enough to believe that men of the cloth or their godly wives cannot have fires lit in them that are not necessarily revival-time fires. The moment I become smug, I'm a wide-open target.

I must acknowledge my own vulnerability. I must exercise discretion. I must recognize the kinds of stones over which I stumble. I must also recognize that the rules God provides are there because God knows what works best in life. When He doesn't tell me, He's trusting my judgment to decide for myself. He doesn't cover up the pitfalls for me, but He expects me to have enough sense to walk around them.

I may also fear because of my husband's occupation. Mark is a pastor. I don't have to look very far to find cases of pastors whose score in fidelity has been in the minus column. My husband counsels people who need help. Many of those people are women. I can dig around in the dirt and find all kinds of examples of romantic relationships that have developed under the guise of counseling. Everyone knows that when people need help, they often become emotionally tied to the person who has provided that help. On the other hand, to feel needed is a tremendous boost to anyone's ego. A few "what if" games based upon a few "it happened" stories, and I'm soon an uptight and jealous wife.

What is the answer? It is not found in a "don't care" attitude, or a feeling of "I'm above it all." Sometimes the higher we are above it all the harder we fall. Nor is the answer found in pitfall paranoia. We may become so obsessed with the potential for stumbling that we create our own potholes. And if I go around trying to cover up the holes of life for my husband, I just might push him into a few. My job is not to cover up the holes for Mark so he doesn't fall in; my job is to provide a safe environment of trust with my husband.

It is interesting that Scripture often implies trust as the antidote for fears. "When I am afraid," David said, "I will trust" (Ps. 56:3). Isaiah also linked the two words together—"I will trust and not be afraid" (Isa. 12:2). Although in both cases the object of trust was God and not a person, the idea of trusting instead of fearing is still there.

What does it mean practically to trust my husband? It means that he will feel the freedom to choose his associates on the basis of their capabilities rather than on their gender because I will not read a physical involvement into every relationship he has with a woman. He will not feel obligated to explain to me why he took his secretary out to lunch or whom he counseled with until ten o'clock last night. He will feel the freedom to reach out to people in warmth and love regardless of who they are because he knows I can differentiate between love and sex. It will be OK for him to need others because he knows that I'm not desperately trying to be everything to him.

The irony of trust is that the more someone trusts me, the more trustworthy I want to be. I remember the feeling of trust that my parents communicated to me when I started to date. I had been in the process of earning their trust before that point, so when the time came for me to start dating, they never discussed curfew with me. It wasn't that they didn't care. What my parents were telling me by their actions was that they believed in me enough to assume I could make responsible decisions for myself. That was a powerful motivation for me to be home at a reasonable hour. The interesting thing about my parents' theory of trust was that it worked. We never had a curfew confrontation. I felt that if they were generous enough to trust me, I would be generous enough to honor their trust.

If, on the other hand, I had felt that my parents expected me to be consistently unreasonable about the time I came home, I probably would not have disappointed them. I probably would have lived up to their expectations and gotten in at unreasonable hours, thinking if they didn't trust me, I might as well give them a legitimate reason for their distrust.

The same principle is true in a marriage. A jealous wife is actually saying that given the right conditions, she predicts her husband will not be able to be faithful to her. Either he is not strong enough to be true, or she is not worth being true to. If a husband is made to feel he is not capable of faithfulness, he may decide that he might as well give his wife a reason to worry. There are always plenty of opportunities.

On the other hand, a trusting wife says to her husband, "I believe in you. The rest is up to you and God." In so doing, she's facing life with the assumption that both God and her husband will keep their promises to her. With a commitment to trust, she has, in a sense, deposited her valuables in God's vault for safekeeping. And if they're in God's safe, she doesn't have to worry; He is responsible for them.

Paul knew what trust was all about. "I am convinced that he [God] is able to guard what I have entrusted to him" (2 Tim. 1:12). So why should I fear? God can protect my valuables for me. I don't need to stand guard by the vault door. I can relax and go on about the business of living free from all the entanglements of a jealous spirit.

When our son Nicky was about three years old, he went with me one day to the savings and loan. As he watched me hand some ten-dollar bills to the stranger on the other side of the teller's window, I could tell by the look on his face that he was greatly distressed. The wise bank teller picked up on Nicky's concern.

"Would you like to see what I'm going to do with your mother's money," he asked. Then, taking Nicky by the hand, he led us down the winding stairs and into the room that housed the vault. As Nicky stood there looking at that two-ton steel door, and hearing the teller explain to him about the iron bars that would close around the metal drawers where his mother's money would be put, I could see my three-year-old release his concern. He sighed deep and long. His mother's money would be safe. He could trust the teller. He could go home in peace. He tucked his hand safely in mine and we walked home in comfort. All was secure.

I have thought of the image over and over in connection with the future of my marriage, the future of my children. God is on duty. He stands even now by that two-ton steel door, keeping watch over what I've placed in the vault. I can go home in peace.

Interaction Time
Personal Reflection

1. On a scale of one to ten, in regard to feelings of trust when it comes to my husband and other women, I would rate myself as a. . . .

2. What reasons do I have for trusting my husband?

3. What reasons do I have for not trusting my husband?
   Are these reasons real or imagined?

4. If real, what steps am I taking or might I take to deal with the reality?

5. If imagined, what steps am I taking or might I take to deal with my imagination?

6. In the past, I have dealt with my jealousies by. . . .

7. I (do, do not) think I handled them in a healthy way because. . . .

8. What do I do that makes it hard on my husband to deal with the women who come into his life and ministry?

9. What do I do that makes it easy on my husband to deal with the women who come into his life and ministry?

10. A time when my husband and I talked about my feelings of jealousy was. . . .

   The result was. . . .
   Next time I would (do it the same, do it differently).
   If I would do it differently next time, *how* would I do it?

11. God's greatest resource for me when I've tended toward jealousy is. . . .
   A Scripture that reminds me of that resource is. . . .

Group Interaction

1. Do you agree that "some jealousy in a marriage relationship can be a good thing"? Why or why not?

2. Do you think a pastor's wife should know the details of her husband's dealings with other women? How much should she ask to know?

3. What would you recommend to a pastor's wife who has concerns about the attention another woman seems to be paying her husband?

4. How does a pastor's wife communicate trust to her husband? How does she communicate distrust?

5. How does she communicate trust for other women in her husband's congregation? How does she communicate distrust?

6. What is the best advice you have either received or given when it comes to feeling relaxed about your husband's counseling ministry with women?

7. What would you consider the greatest safeguard a ministerial couple can build into their marriage?

8. Think of a ministerial couple you know or have heard of who apparently have a marriage built on trust. Describe what you know of that marriage.

9. What suggestions do you have for building a marriage on trust?

10. What biblical principles apply to the issue of trusting your husband? What Scripture references apply?

11. How would you pray for another pastor's wife who is struggling with the issue of trusting her husband in his ministry to women? Verbalize that prayer right now.

EIGHT

What Do I Have to Feel
Guilty About?
Learning to Say No

She was a shining example of a pastor's wife—totally involved in
the work of the church, giving herself sacrificially to its meetings, its programs, and its outreach. She was a spotless example
of motherhood—five children who were all well-behaved, well-
adjusted, well-dressed, and following in the blameless example
of their mother and father. She was the ultimate in hospitality—ten for dinner on Saturday night, six college students and
a retired college professor for dinner on Sunday, fifty for a
buffet in honor of the church missionaries. She was dedication
personified—in the church kitchen every month cooking meals
for 150 of the community's senior citizens, up at 5:00 A.M. to
attend an early morning prayer meeting down at the church

with her husband, speaking to groups of women about what it was like to be a pastor's wife, fixing dinner for a sick youth director's wife. The list went on.

As I sat and listened to her speak that day, I felt myself getting weak-kneed just mentally trying to keep up with all she did. What am I doing even pretending to play the game, I thought to myself? Suddenly, I wasn't sure I was even in the game. By definition I was very much in the arena, but when it came to scoring the points, I was beginning to feel like I was way out in the stands somewhere. If hers was the standard, I simply was not making it when it came to being a pastor's wife. I had adequate proof from comparing myself with what I was hearing.

I left the meeting that day with a colossal guilt complex. It was a complex so complex that it took me days to work through. I simply was not enough of anything. I was not dedicated enough. I was not spiritual enough. I was not sacrificial enough. I was not caring enough. I was not hospitable enough. I was not anything enough.

Slowly and somewhat painfully I was able to work myself out from under the huge load of guilt I had dumped upon myself that day. "Now what is it exactly that I have to feel guilty about?" I asked. I went right down the list.

Should I feel guilty about the fact that I was not the organized, efficient, easy-going mother of five. Mark and I had decided long ago that two was the size that fit us perfectly when it came to family. I crossed that one off the list.

Should I feel guilty because I didn't make it to the 6:00 A.M. prayer meetings down at the church? Baby-sitters just aren't very plentiful at that hour of the morning, and my children were not old enough to baby-sit each other. I crossed that one off the list.

Should I feel guilty that I wasn't in the church kitchen once a month cooking dinner for 150 senior citizens? It was all I could do to get dinner on the table for six guests and still maintain my equilibrium without totally destroying the sanity of the three people who live with me. Feats of culinary strength were just not my hallmark. I crossed that one off the list.

By the time I had worked through the list, I had deposited all my reasons for guilt into the not guilty column. There was not one single thing that my model pastor's wife had said that morning that was a legitimate reason for me to feel guilty.

Where does my guilt come from? If I want to find things about which I can feel guilty, comparing myself with someone else always works very well. When I hear that my friend spent the afternoon ice skating with her children, I immediately think of what my children are missing because their mother did not take them ice skating. They are deprived because their mother is either too busy, too ungiving, or too uninterested in her kids. That invokes enough guilt to keep me going for awhile. For me, comparisons always come packaged with guilt. If I don't want the guilt, then I'd better not compare myself with others.

Another time when I land in the garbage dump of guilt is when I do not distinguish between what is real guilt and what is imagined guilt.

There is a legitimate guilt. When I deliberately ignore what God has spelled out for me in black and white, unless I am totally calloused and insensitive to sin, I will feel guilty. It is God's way of prodding me to set the record straight. If I do not feel guilt for what is clearly a violation of God's standard, I'm headed for trouble.

The problem comes when I feel guilty about that which God never intended me to feel guilty. Guilt over not taking my children skating or not having a candlelight dinner for two on Mark's birthday, even though one of my friends did that for her husband, are not legitimate reasons for guilt. They have nothing whatsoever to do with sin in my life. They do not necessarily mean that I am not interested in the happiness of my children or my husband. They do not necessarily mean that I am a self-centered person. And yet, to legitimize my guilt, I will assign some spiritual flaw to my character. Then I have created an excuse to wallow in my guilt.

Most guilt in my life is not God-imposed, but self-imposed. It does not come from deliberate sin, but from my own insecurities. It does not come from failing to meet God's standards, but from failing to meet my own standards or the standards I think others have set for me. It is then that guilt becomes a destructive force in my life.

I remember vividly my bout with guilt when I started staying home from Wednesday evening prayer meeting. Pastors' wives just don't miss Wednesday night prayer meeting. All my life I had gone to church on Wednesday night; it was as natural as eating and sleeping. But things changed when we had children. My dilemma ended with guilt whichever way I turned. If I made my children crabby because I kept them from their normal bedtime, I felt guilty. If I left them with a baby-sitter, I felt guilty for leaving them another night of the week. If I stayed home I felt guilty, because if the pastor's wife didn't show up for prayer meeting, why should anyone else? It took a long time for me to give myself permission to stay home. And once I had given myself permission, it was a long time before I could stay home and not feel guilty about it.

I finally resolved it when I could accept the fact that staying home from prayer meeting is not breaking one of the Ten Commandments. It does not mean that I'm slipping spiritually. It does not mean I'm a prayer dropout. It does not mean I'm not a faithful, dedicated pastor's wife. For me, staying home from prayer meeting on Wednesday nights means that my children are at a stage in their lives when they need to be home being tucked into bed by their mother more than they need to be running wild around the church while Mother tries to pray.

Another destructive imprint that guilt stamps upon my life is that I live apologetically. This occurs when guilt becomes a habit and I assume a my-fault attitude before all the facts are even in.

"I'm sorry" is a handy phrase to have around. It has mended many a broken fence for me. But there are times when I use it far more than necessary.

One day I found myself apologizing to my neighbor because she had to walk over a snowdrift in my backyard to get to my house. "You don't have to be sorry. You didn't send the blizzard," was her response.

There are a lot of times I have to realize that I didn't cause the blizzard. Things are not always my fault. There just may be other factors involved. But I'm blinded to those other factors when I automatically assume I'm to blame. I often take far more of the responsibility for things than God ever intended.

If someone leaves the church, I remember that I never invited them over for dinner. Indirectly I am saying that they left the church because of my lack of hospitality. If a woman in the congregation leaves her husband and family, I wonder if I was not available enough to that woman to help prevent the crash.

I often fall into the same trap with my children. If Nicky is naughty in Sunday School, I will go home and look over my calendar from last week to see if I was gone too much. If Jori and Nicky are constantly fighting, I immediately check out when I last sat down and played with them.

If we always need neat little answers to life's perplexing situations, we must fix the blame on something or someone. However, life cannot always be tied up in a neat little "here's why" package. Nicky may be naughty simply because he is three-and-a-half-year-old Nicky. Nicky and Jori may be fighting just because brothers and sisters fight. It may have nothing whatsoever to do with me.

The problem with making myself the scapegoat is that although I may get away with it for things which are of minor consequence, when some earth-shattering crisis comes along, the weight of that responsibility is far greater than I can bear.

I remember hearing the story of a young missionary mother who suffered a mental and emotional collapse following the drowning of her three-year-old in their backyard wading pool. She never forgot the fact that she had walked over to visit her neighbor just before the drowning occurred. In her eyes she was as guilty for her daughter's death as if she had murdered her. Assuming too much personal responsibility for life is a dangerous way to live.

One of the more dramatic moments in my life came when I was having lunch with a friend one afternoon. I watched the blood literally drain from her face when she answered the telephone and received the message that her father had been found dead on the garage floor; his car was still running. Cheryl and I arrived just as the paramedics were loading him into the ambulance.

Immediately the memories came pouring in. We had spent Sunday evening with him just two weeks earlier. Things had seemed so normal, so right. We had talked about a lot of things that night. Evidently, we had not talked about the right things.

"Never mind how he died," the pastor said at the funeral. "Remember how he lived." I remembered. He was on the church board, the Christian education committee, and was the Sunday School superintendent. We thought we knew him. Evidently we didn't. We thought we were his friends. Why didn't he lean on his friends? He had had ample opportunity to tell us. Why didn't he feel free? We were close to him and yet evidently not close enough.

I agonized over that death for a long time. I finally found freedom by accepting the fact that Mark and I had been his friends. We had not let him down. We had been as open and honest and loving with him as we had known how. I knew I had to forget about what I could have done and think about what I had done for him. I was not responsible for the fact that he felt he could no longer face life. Mark was not responsible. Cheryl was not responsible. His wife was not responsible. I didn't know who or what was, but I decided to leave that up to God. I could no longer carry the load.

The frightening thing about my guilt feelings over my friend's death was that if I felt that deeply involved with a friend's death, what would happen if it were my own flesh and blood. I feared for my own stability. I began to realize how devastating guilt could be. And I was convinced that was not what God had in mind for me.

I'm a person who will always feel deeply. I find myself crawling inside of people's skins whether I want to or not. I feel for them. I cry for them. I care for them. But I cannot go around bearing the responsibility for them. I will love them, be available to them, stand with them, steady them, support them. But should they go under, I will not drown with them. Their destiny belongs to them and God.

I am not a cause. I am an influence. That means I am

concerned about my relationships with people. I recognize that part of me rubs off on those I touch. That is enough to make me cautious; it makes me responsible *to* people, but not responsible *for* them.

The moment I become a cause, I am carrying more weight than God intended me to carry. God doesn't even work that way with me. He doesn't assume the responsibility for me. He puts the burden upon me and upon the choices I make. So why should I assume the responsibility for others when even God who is all-powerful does not do that for me?

Another contribution that guilt makes to my life is that it saps me of my strength to say no. If I always feel guilty about saying no I will say yes in order to avoid the guilt. Guilt makes me uncomfortable so I say yes to relieve my discomfort. Thus, I can easily find myself doing things out of guilt rather than out of conviction that this is what I should be doing. Feeling guilty may cut short my rational, decision-making process. When I am guided by my emotions rather than my mind, I end up doing things I'm not equipped to do—either from a time or ability standpoint.

For example, I was very uncomfortable when I heard that out of a church of over 2,000 people, our church staff could not find enough women who were willing to be a pal to one of the 150 girls in our Pioneer Girl program. I was even more uncomfortable when I received the sign-up sheet after it had passed through a Sunday School class of over 100 people and there were only six names on the list. I furiously signed my name and turned in the sheet.

The next week's mail included a list of the year's activities for Pioneer Girl pals. I had a conflict on the very first date. By the time I went down the list, there were more dates that I could not keep than dates that I could. Suddenly I remembered my priority list. I had drawn it up before the year began so I would know when to say no. It was funny how quickly I forgot about it when guilt took over. Being a Pioneer Girl pal was not on my list of priorities for the year.

It was much more embarrassing for me to have to call the head of the committee and back down on my commitment than it would have been to simply pass the list on without signing. It was far more humiliating to have to ask someone to take my place because I had over-committed myself than it would have been to have simply said, "I'm sorry, I'm already committed to all I can handle for the year." My guilt had taken me down a road I never should have taken, and it cost me a great amount of time and energy to retrace my steps.

Guilt feelings can also lead me to act inconsistently. If I am feeling guilty about something, I will tend to overcompensate just to relieve my guilt. If, for example, I feel that I have been too hard on Jori in my disciplining of her, my guilt will lead me to be much easier on her the next time. Guilt clouds the picture. Soon the degree of discipline Jori receives is equal to the degree of my guilt feelings at the moment rather than to the degree of seriousness of the offense. Sometimes I find myself performing the same routine with my involvement in the church. One Sunday morning a friend casually mentioned to me that one of my neighbors who had just started coming to our church was feeling very lonely. I took the casual remark very personally. After all, she was my neighbor. I immediately decided I must launch a neighborly crusade.

On the way out of church that morning, I ran into one of our young single interns. I knew he lived alone and did his own cooking so I asked him to join us for dinner. That afternoon I called and invited the new neighbor over for dinner Saturday night. On Monday I whipped up a coffee cake and ran it over to another neighbor who was moving to Florida the next day. On Wednesday I took a young widow with four children to a luncheon with me. Saturday night I entertained my guests. By Sunday I was wiped out.

I enjoy being neighborly. I enjoy taking people to luncheons and feeding hungry interns and baking coffee cakes for neighbors. But I enjoy them much more when I take them at a sane pace. I also enjoy helping others more when I do it for the sheer pleasure and not because a prick of guilt has sent me into orbit.

It is one thing to be guilty. It is another to feel guilty. The writer of 1 John appears to be drawing this distinction when he says that we can be free from guilt even when we feel guilty because God is greater than our feelings. "We set our hearts at rest in His presence whenever our hearts condemn us. For God is greater than our hearts, and He knows everything" (1 John 3:19-20).

God says I am not guilty. I do not need to live under the canopy of condemnation. That's what the Cross is all about. "Therefore, there is now no condemnation for those who are in Christ Jesus" (Rom. 8:1). "For God did not send his Son into the world to condemn the world, but to save the world through him" (John 3:17). God doesn't ignore my mistakes. But He does stamp the record "paid in full." "Neither do I condemn you. . . . Go now and leave your life of sin," is His benediction upon me just as it was upon the adulterous woman (John 8:11). Why should I not walk free from guilt?

What is the result of guilt-free living? "If our hearts do not condemn us, we have confidence before God" (1 John 3:21). It is not God's will that we shrink from life and hide in the shadows of guilt. His will is that we face Him and face our world with heads held high because He has declared us "not guilty."

As a Christian, I, of all people, should be able to live guilt-free. And if I am guilt-free, I will be confident. I will not need to compare myself with others. I will not approach life from a feeling of deficiency but from a feeling of adequacy because God has made me adequate. I will not need to take on the destiny of another's life. God is in control of that person's life just as He is in control of mine. I will have boldness to say no when life asks from me more than I can give. And I will not need to apologize or timidly mumble my excuses. Rather my "no" can be graciously emphatic because I am certain about the direction I should take. Guilt-free living enables me to do what I can do without worrying about all I cannot or am not doing.

On the other hand, God-imposed guilt is an important check in my life. Divine guilt leads to recognition and confession of sin. Without it I would soon become calloused to wrong. I would have no accountability. No spiritual check. Guilt therefore, when it is God-imposed, rather than self-imposed is a valuable asset to my walk of faith.

Interaction Time
Personal Reflection

1. If someone asked, I would have to say, guilt (is, is not) a major force in my life.

2. The times I do feel guilty, I suspect the guilt is (God-imposed, self-imposed). The reason I suspect this is. . . .

3. If I would have to do a spot check of my life for self-imposed guilt, I would have to say its symptoms show up in the following ways. . . .

4. A time when I felt guilty over something I did not need to feel guilty about, was when. . . .
If I had it to do over again, I would. . . .

5. A time when I felt legitimate guilt as God's means of nudging me toward confession was when. . . .

6. If I had to analyze my self-imposed guilt, I suspect it might come from. . . .

7. I have felt guilt in relation to my role as pastor's wife in the following ways:

8. I suspect the reason I feel guilty concerning my role is because. . . .

9. If I were to ask someone to pray for me concerning the guilt I sometimes feel I would ask them to pray for help in the following specific areas:

10. One step I need to take to deal with my feelings of guilt is. . . .

Group Interaction
1. Do you agree that some guilt is necessary in our lives? Explain your answer.

2. Do you agree that pastors' wives have more to feel guilty about than most wives? Explain.

3. How have you seen guilt impact pastors' wives?

4. How has guilt impacted your own life?

5. How can one know the difference between self-imposed and God-imposed guilt?

6. What are some steps one might take to overcome self-imposed guilt?

7. What are some Scripture references that relate to guilt?

8. As far as God is concerned, how does one go about living free from the condemnation of guilt?

9. If you had to give pastors' wives one piece of advice relating to guilt, what would it be?

10. How might another pastor's wife help you when it comes to dealing with guilt in your life? If guilt is not an issue in your life, what might you do to help someone in whose life it is an issue?

11. What would you pray for another who is struggling under a weight of guilt? Take time to verbalize the prayer to God right now.

NINE

Help! I'm Lonely
Learning to Need Others

"I know you're very busy and you probably don't need another night out, but we're going to stick our neck out anyway and invite you and Mark over for dinner." My prospective hostess seemed surprised when I answered, "Yes, we do need another night out." Joy not only picked up the cue that we needed a dinner invitation, but also the cue that I needed a friend.

We had been on staff at the church for a year. It had been a year of hectic motion—change, adjustments, meeting people, finding niches, learning to feel comfortable. We were invited out. We invited people in. We went from meeting to meeting, activity to activity. We feasted on potlucks, picnics, luncheons, and late evening coffees. We had climbed aboard a fast-moving train.

I hung on tenaciously and moved with the motion. Outwardly, things were traveling full steam ahead. But inwardly, under all the noise, there were the sounds of silence. I had left my feelings in another place. They were with my friends from the church we had been in for the last seven years. In the new situation I had filled my silence with noise, my emptiness with activity, but I felt alone in all the flurry.

"I don't know why I'm so amazed that you feel lonely sometimes too," was my new friend's comment when I finally got brave enough to admit to her that I was very lonely. "I've always thought of you as having plenty to do. I guess I thought because you're busy you aren't lonely."

As I thought about Joy's comment on my busyness, I came to the conclusion that one of the reasons I was lonely might be that I was so busy. There was always business to take care of, services to attend, projects to support, lessons to teach. I rushed by with my "Hi, how are you" and smiled at people long-distance as I entered and exited from church.

I was so busy meeting people that I never had time to get to know anyone. I was so occupied with planning programs that would lift their souls that I couldn't squeeze in an hour to sit down and find out what was going on inside their souls. I gave my performances. I taught my lessons. But who knew what I was really feeling down deep inside. I was surrounded by people, but close to no one. I listened to so many that I couldn't hear anyone. And then I wondered why I was lonely.

Another conclusion I've come to about loneliness is that movement does not heal it—neither does close physical proximity. Loneliness is not cured by simply being with a person.

Carol and I were a team during the days when my life centered around youth work. Whatever needed to be done, we did well together. Our personalities meshed. Our abilities complemented each other. We spent a lot of time together, and our finished products were always to our credit.

When Carol moved out of state and I went to visit her, I suddenly realized that in our two years together I had never really gotten to know Carol. If someone had asked me to describe her, I could have given a complete list of the externals—

how she looked, what she did. But I didn't know much about how she felt, what she feared, liked, disliked, dreamed about, hoped for. It was when we no longer had our activities to draw us together that we got beyond what we did to what we really felt. For the first time we sensed not just a business partnership, but a true companionship as we opened some inside doors to each other. That potential for companionship had been there all along, but we had allowed our activity to become a substitute for it. And when activity becomes a substitute for intimacy, we're lonely.

Busyness may contribute to my loneliness, but being busy does not necessarily mean I will be lonely. However, I may create my own aloneness if I give others the impression that I'm busy. When people always have to apologize to me for interrupting me or bothering me, or always start their phone conversations with "I know you're busy but . . ." I probably should think twice about the image I'm projecting to others. If they get the impression that I'm a very busy person, they probably won't risk interrupting me and being rejected. They would rather play it safe and leave me alone. A steady diet of being left alone because people think I'm too busy to be interrupted, and I'm soon starving to death from lack of companionship.

I have watched busy people and have observed two kinds— people who are in fact busy but do not appear to be, and people who appear to be busy but really aren't. It seems to me that not all busy people are lonely, but people who impress others with their busyness often are.

I have a friend who has an amazing capacity for daily production, yet she never makes me feel her busyness. When I talk to her, I have no idea that she has twenty-four things on her list to accomplish by midnight tonight. She does not keep looking at her watch. She looks straight at me. She doesn't flip open her datebook or tell me how many nights she's been out in the past week. She doesn't walk fast or always have a pile of manila folders under her arm. She isn't mentally fifty paces ahead of me when I talk to her. I know because she can always repeat back to me what I've just said to her, and she often does just to let me know she's listening.

Perhaps that's why she knows a lot about me. I feel safe in telling her what's going on inside me because I don't have to compete with her schedule. She gives me the impression that she has all the time in the world for me.

I know my friend has her lonely times. She's told me so. But I also know that she has an amazing capacity to care about people, and consequently many people care about her. Her life is full of warm, loving relationships with people.

Another reason for loneliness is my predisposition to serve people. Call it genes, environmental conditioning, biblical mandate, or pastor's-wife-itis, but it can make me a very willing giver and a very unwilling receiver. When I cannot allow another to give to me, I've got a one-sided relationship, and one-sided relationships can be lonely relationships.

There have been times when I've wanted to say, "Hey, I'm lonely. Let me tell you about it." Sometimes I've said it. More often I've listened to others say it. Some days I've needed a hand to hold and a shoulder to cry on. More often I've said, "Here's my shoulder. You may cry on it. Here's my hand. I'll help you along." Sometimes I've wanted to say, "Hey, someone, allow me to struggle. Stand with me if I fail." More often I've said, "Go ahead and struggle. I'll stand with you if you fail." There have been the Sunday mornings when I've felt, "Someone, please look behind my open hymnbook and my Bible and find me." More often I have looked behind open hymnbooks and Bibles and said, "Tell me how things are for you today."

Yes, there have been listening ears in my life, and strong shoulders and sure hands and safe sides to walk by me. But usually, I haven't given myself permission to use them. I have, instead, assumed that I must be the ears and hands and shoulders. I have assumed that I must be strong for them. I am their helper, supporter, friend, and servant.

Where did we ever get the notion that ministers can't be ministered to? We didn't get it from Jesus. He washed His disciples' feet, but He also allowed them to wash His feet (John 12–13). Could it be that we are so busy washing other people's feet that we fail to see the need for letting others wash our feet;

that we see ourselves only as ministers and not as those to whom someone else can minister; that we wrap our cloak of loneliness more tightly around us by not allowing ourselves to need people? Perhaps we are creating lofty, lonely positions for ourselves by eliminating our need for others?

I have often found myself involved with people during crisis passages in their lives—death, divorce, mental illness, suicide of a loved one. I have cared, and I have been a friend. But my relationships with people in crisis cannot be two-dimensional. I cannot lay on them even a small portion of the load I'm carrying, for their own load is great enough.

Therefore, I've found that my friendships with people in crisis cannot be the only ones I have. These are important relationships to me, but there are times when I need comfort too.

It took me a long time to realize that I needed a friend with whom there could be mutual load-bearing. Slowly, I began to associate my comforter-complex with loneliness. I realized that life cannot be a steady diet of being a friend to others. I needed the nourishment of allowing someone to be a friend to me.

There is a myth about the pastor's wife that contributed to my lonely times during the first years of marriage. I never read it in a book or heard a seminar that was built around it, and no pastor's wife ever spelled it out for me in terms of advice. But somewhere along the line I picked up the idea that a pastor's wife had to be a friend to all and close companion to none. Somewhere I got the picture that the church was full of people who were just waiting for the chance to be friends with the pastor's wife. In order to be fair to everyone and not have anyone get jealous over the fact that they were not my friend too, I would have to be friends to everyone.

That kind of thinking did a lot for my ego. I handed out my friendship like it was an award that people were eagerly waiting to receive. I had to be careful that I did not give out my prize unless I had enough to go around or someone would be hurt and terribly disappointed.

Now, I'll admit that the church is full of cliques, and I do not want to be in a clique. I do not want to have my eyes on

one person and miss everyone else around me. I do not want to
come to church on Sunday morning and sit with the same
person week after week, month after month, year after year.
Things can get pretty narrow if we go out with the same couple
for dinner every week or limit our calls to one phone number.
That kind of social existence is not healthy for anyone. But it is
possible to have close friendships without having cliques.

My fantasy about the value of my friendship and my dislike
for cliques gave me plenty of reasons for my equal-friendships-
with-everyone-routine in the first church in which Mark
served. I came away from five years of associations with lots of
names on my list to whom I would send Christmas cards each
year; but there was no one on that list whom I felt free to drop
in on for a night if I happened to be back in the area, or call
long-distance and say "Help!"

That first church was not a cold, unfriendly church. There
were many young wives with whom I had common denominators, and there were a number of people with whom I could
have had close ties. But I refused to allow myself to get tied in
with anyone in particular for fear of the congregation in general. As a result, those years were lonely.

In looking back over those years of no-close-friends-from-the-
church policy, I think another factor was probably involved. I
was a new bride. I had Mark, my lifelong friend and lover. He
encouraged, comforted, informed, loved, and served. He allowed me to do the same for him. Why should I need anyone
else in the congregation or even in the whole world?

As the magical spell of "he is all I need" began to fade, I
realized that no matter how sensitive, gentle, loving, and insightful my lifelong friend and lover was, he was not all I
needed. Sometimes I needed others too.

Needing close friends did not detract from the value of
Mark's friendship or mean that he was failing me. It just meant
that I needed different kinds of friendships and that God could
touch my life through many different relationships.

I believe that God created us with needs for intimacy—
companionship, warmth, love, nearness. He knew aloneness
was not good. That's why He created a companion for Adam.

I need special relationships. They are God's way of entering my lonely times. But I also believe I need to build my friendships with care. I dare not cheapen them by trying to duplicate my friendships with everyone who comes along. Mass distribution cheapens the product. Not everyone should be my close friend. Nor can I afford to abuse my friendships by exploiting them, or flaunting them, or breaking confidences, or becoming possessive. As I see God's care and love for me put into the flesh of a friend, I cannot help but reach out for it with happiness, thankfulness, and carefulness.

I have always been intrigued by the kind of friendship that Paul exhibited through his letters to his friends. His correspondence to the Philippians is one example. In it I see the qualities of friendship that attract me to a person, the qualities I want to give to others through my friendship with them.

"I have you in my heart," Paul said to his friends. "I thank my God every time I remember you. In all my prayers for . . . you, I always pray with joy because of your partnership. . . . I am glad and rejoice with all of you. So you too should be glad and rejoice with me" (Phil. 1:3-5; 2:17-18).

Paul knew about nearness. Evidently he felt the human urges to be with his friends and knew the emptiness when he couldn't be with them. He didn't say, "If I ever come your way, I'll drop by." He said, "I long for all of you" (Phil. 1:8).

Paul anticipated being with his friends. "I am confident in the Lord that I myself will come soon [to you]" (Phil. 2:24). I believe Paul was the kind of friend who would have driven an extra hundred miles or caught a midnight flight just so he could spend time with a friend. He would probably have checked in by phone when he was away for long periods of time, just to see how things were going, rather than send a mimeographed form letter at Christmas. I get the impression that Paul knew how to give himself to his friends.

I see in Paul an honesty and openness. He told his friends about his joys, his hopes, his expectations, his desires, his goals, his values. He was willing to let them know when he was hard-pressed and when he couldn't figure out exactly how he felt (Phil. 1:22-24). He allowed them to see his conflicts and told them about his imperfections (Phil. 1:30; 3:12-13).

Paul was not afraid to need what the Philippians could offer to him. He encouraged them to give and he received their gifts as a "fragrant aroma" of God's love and care for him (Phil. 4:18). Paul seems to have realized that though he was a strong leader, he could not go it alone. He needed his friends and the tangible and intangible gifts they could give to him.

Paul not only sensed that he needed his friends, but also that they needed him. He took their gifts, but he also gave gifts to them. He saw their potential and called forth the best in them (Phil. 1:6). Paul's confidence in them probably helped to inspire confidence in themselves.

Paul gave advice to his friends when they needed it; he gave warning when they needed it (Phil. 3:1-3). He was not afraid of touchy situations and called the tensions by name when he felt they needed correction (Phil. 4:2). His love included the things they were doing right and the things they were doing wrong. He cared enough to be honest with them.

I feel that Paul would be the kind of friend who could see my hidden gifts and gently draw them from me and inspire in me the confidence to offer my gifts to the world. He would also give me his advice, his insights, his rebukes. And he would allow me the freedom to give the same to him. As far as I'm concerned, that's the kind of companionship I need in this impersonal, high-speed world in which I live.

Interaction Time
Personal Reflection
    1. Which of the following is most nearly true of me?
        ___ I would describe myself as basically a lonely person.
        ___ I sometimes feel lonely but do not feel I am basically a lonely person.

    2. Observations I have made about myself when I am feeling lonely are. . . .

    3. Sometimes I mask my loneliness by. . . .
       A time I did this was when. . . .

Consequences were. . . .
Next time I would do it differently by. . . .

4. Agree/Disagree? I basically am willing to admit when I am lonely.

5. If I have trouble admitting to loneliness, one reason might be. . . .

6. One thing I might be doing to cause my own loneliness is. . . .

7. If I asked a trusted friend to evaluate me in terms of my approachability, I think she might say. . . .

8. If lack of approachability is one thing that keeps people from me and me from people, something I might change is. . . .

9. One way I might let others know I need them is. . . .

10. If I had to describe the kinds of friendships I have I would say. . . .

11. I (am, am not) basically satisfied with the level of intimacy I have reached in my friendships.

12. One reason developing and maintaining friendships has been (hard, easy) for me may be. . . .

13. One step I need to take as a result of reading the chapter is. . . .

Group Interaction
1. Do you think pastors' wives in general have a harder time with friendships? Why or why not?

2. Share an example of a quality friendship you have experienced. What about that person made her especially valuable to you as a pastor's wife?

3. Do you think pastors' wives in general have a harder time letting people help them? Why or why not?

4. Why do you think loneliness is the number one feeling pastors' wives have admitted to having?

5. What is the difference in being alone and being lonely? When have you felt both and coped successfully?

6. What ideas might you share concerning how to compensate for times you are alone?

7. Do you agree or disagree with the statement, "a pastor and his wife should always be a step ahead of the people in their congregation?" Explain.

8. Why do you suppose the "pedestal" image is sometimes used to describe the pastor and his family? Do you think it is an accurate portrayal of most pastoral families? Do you think it is a healthy reality for pastors and their families? Why or why not?

9. When has loneliness been a destructive force in your life? How did you overcome?

10. Do you think pastors' wives sometimes create their own alienation? In what ways?

11. What advice would you give to pastors' wives struggling with feelings of alienation and loneliness?

12. What biblical principles and passages would you use to encourage pastors' wives who feel alone? What specific qualities would you ask God to give them?

TEN

Two for the Price of One
Learning about Priorities

We were being interviewed for a position in a new church. I followed Mark through the maze of meetings, stood by his side in reception lines, gave my testimony before the church board, and answered any questions put to me. I related my past, present, and future expectations. I told them about my education, my career, my involvement in church ministry, my interests, my hobbies, my likes and dislikes. I made statements about my theology, my philosophy of life, and my goals.

And then came the clincher. "Some churches hire a man. Some hire a team and pay a man. Do you consider Mark's ministry *his* job or *our* job?" I complimented my interviewer on his skillfully worded question. He had given me no hint of the answer he wanted to hear. I wasn't sure whether this church hired a man or a team. I decided it really didn't matter. He had asked an honest question; I should give an honest answer.

My honest answer is not something I thought up overnight or came to while I was singing in the shower. It is a progression of stages through which I have passed and continue to pass in my quest for oneness with Mark and yet distinctiveness which allows me to use my God-given gifts to be the unique person God made me.

It is never a simple exercise for a wife to figure out exactly how she should relate to her husband's job. If she views it as his job, she may easily become aloof from it, passive toward it, or disinterested in it. If, on the other hand, she assumes that it is *our* job, she may throw herself into what he is and lose herself in the process. Either extreme has its dangers.

Sometimes we have problems with the idea of oneness. When God says that husband and wife are to be one flesh (Gen. 2:24), we assume that we have to decide whose flesh, whose career, whose schedule, whose interests, and whose activities. For awhile I assumed I was to be Mark.

Our interview for Mark's first church position was almost over. "Of course you know we are hiring you so we can get your wife," the pastor laughed as he saw us to the door. We all laughed. He was a good friend of mine who, along with his family, had befriended me during my college days in a big city far from home. Obviously, he was hiring Mark because he felt Mark was capable of handling the job. But he did get me thrown in, whether he wanted it that way or not. I considered myself a package deal with Mark.

And package deal we were. We were the youth minister; Mark was the male part of the youth minister, and I was the female part. Mark led the meetings; I hostessed the meetings. Mark directed the plays; I wrote the scripts. Mark counseled and led Bible studies with the guys; I counseled and led Bible studies with the girls. Mark performed the weddings; I performed service in the kitchen or spoke to the bride at the bridal shower. There was usually some way I could plug into whatever Mark had to do.

I was totally immersed in his job. When the church needed another secretary, I volunteered for the job. It was the perfect setup. We lived next door to the church. I had completed one stage of my college education and felt I needed a breather before going on. Mark and I could have breakfast, lunch, and dinner together. I could take notes for him at his meetings, type his letters, run errands with him, greet his visitors, answer his phone, and open his mail. We were a team all the way.

I knew Mark's every move for almost every moment of the day. I knew when he was having a cup of coffee, when he was talking on the phone, when he was studying for a sermon, or when he took a walk down the hall. I knew when parents called to complain about a youth group activity or when the church staff was having some trouble getting along with each other. I also was painfully aware when Mark and I weren't getting along. We could never get away from it.

I worried over the details of "our" job. I gave reminders and made appointments. I juggled my work load to keep everyone happy. I clucked away like a mother hen. It was our job, and I was half of the team. No one could accuse me of being a passive pastor's wife.

But it wasn't long before our neat little package-deal, youth minister team began to feel some strain. We were being smothered by each other's presence. I was Mark's wife, lover, phone service, script writer, typist, friend, cook, errand girl, secretary, and date. Now that is a good way to get very tired of someone in a big hurry.

My zealous involvement in Mark's work began to boomerang. "She's trying so hard to help me out, she must feel I'm not capable of running things on my own," was the feeling I began to project to Mark. It did a lot for my ego to be needed so much, but it wasn't exactly strengthening Mark's.

We decided that if we wanted to go on living together, we'd better stop working together. I went back to school, and Mark went on with his business of being a youth director. And we enjoyed each other much more at the end of the day.

Our marriage seems to be healthier when we maintain a healthy distance from each other's jobs. A healthy distance from my husband's job doesn't mean I'm distant from my husband. It doesn't mean I'm disinterested or uninvolved or unsupportive. It doesn't mean I become an island to myself or that I am preoccupied with my interests and my job. It simply means that I acknowledge that Mark is competent in his own right as a pastor. He does not need a duplication or a female counterpart to make him worth the amount of his salary. He doesn't need someone to dot his i's and cross his liturgical t's for him. He is the pastor. I am not.

Another problem that arises when a wife assumes responsibility for her husband's job is that she usually ends up working four or five jobs—her husband's, her own, plus being wife, mother, homemaker. Now if you are superwoman or don't care about wearing yourself out by the ripe old age of forty, that's all right. Many Christians assume that if they wear themselves out for the Lord it's OK: "It is better to burn out than to rust out."

But I don't want to do either. And yet I found myself burning out. I went from the package-deal approach to a high-powered auxiliary program. I plunged in. I packed my moments full. I defied the laws of nature and then depended on the Holy Spirit's power to pull me through. It was Mark's job, yes. But it was my responsibility to fully participate.

And participate I did, even with Jori on the scene. A baby slowed me down for about one week. Then she climbed right on board the merry-go-round with me. At that point I wasn't sure how I felt about mothers working outside the home, but I sure was in favor of mothers working in the church, especially when your husband got paid by the church.

If my husband's job happens to be labeled "God's service," I have double reason why his work should be mine. If I say I don't have time to serve on the Christian Education committee or teach in Vacation Bible School, I'm not only saying no to my husband; I'm saying no to God. And that's serious business.

So how do I work through the complexities of relating to my husband's job. How do I translate "one flesh" into hours and minutes? How do I deal with the fact that God has put a talent into my hand and will return some day to see what I've done with that talent. Does he expect me to have buried my talent and helped someone else double his (Matt. 25)?

Several things have helped me in my struggle to deal with these questions. One is that I must respect the physical laws of nature. My body is put together in such a way that it has its own built-in tolerance level. When I push myself beyond that level, my body will tell me so. Trying to carry four or five jobs at one time is one way to set the alarm ringing.

When I've exceeded my maximum capacity, I get tired, discouraged, passive. I go and sit down under my juniper tree like Elijah did (1 Kings 19) and say, "Lord, I've been so zealous for You and look what I get in return. Besides that, I've blown it. No one needs me. No one is standing with me. Let's just get this show over with." I want to close myself in my cave or run for the wilderness. The future looks gloomy, the past tragic. The present seems impossible. I search furiously for God in the wind, the earthquake, and the fire, but I do not find Him.

God comes to me and says, "Here, Ruth. Lie down under this juniper tree and get some sleep. Eat this food, for the journey is too great for you. Get off your mountaintop, out of the wind, the earthquake, the fire. Sit at the door of your cave and find Me in the sound of a 'gentle whisper' (1 Kings 19:12). Don't let your zeal for Me cause the collapse of the temple in which I dwell" (1 Cor. 6:19, 20). I have come to realize that I don't need to do all God's work. There are other people who can do it too. Isn't that what the body of Christ is all about— ears, eyes, feet working together (1 Cor. 12)? Sometimes we think we have to be the whole body. But why should we deny someone else the opportunity to use his or her gifts?

Moses had the same problem. He was the leader of the Israelites. That meant he had to be their bread man, their Culligan water man, their travel guide, their psychologist, their priest, and their judge. His father-in-law finally had to say, "Moses, what are you doing? You are wearing yourself out. The job is too heavy for you; you can't do it alone. Let others help you" (Ex. 18:14-24). Moses was wise enough to heed his advice.

I have come to the conclusion that the question concerning Mark's career and how I relate to it is not "his job or our job" but "how do I invest my time?"

A wise person knows how to use her time; she plans ahead. Jesus once told a story which emphasizes the point. He called five women foolish because they forgot to include lamp oil on the week's shopping list and consequently missed the party because they had to run out and buy some at the last minute (Matt. 25:1-12).

Knowing how to use my time includes setting priorities. My list of priorities must be based on what I value. For example, I value the stability of my family life. I also value the people in the church. However, I know, that I will be living the rest of my life with my family. It is unlikely that I will spend the rest of my life with the people of this particular church. Therefore, I will spend more time on things that concern my family than on things that concern the church simply because my relationship with my family is more permanent than my relationship with the people of the church.

I also know enough about my nature to know that I am basically self-centered. I would enjoy spending all my time on me and the things I value most. God knows that about human nature too. Perhaps that's why He suggested to Moses in the Old Testament that His people bring a tenth of their possessions and give it to Him.

To me, the tithe represents a kind of balance between giving nothing at all and feeling that we have to give all. God didn't say, "Give what you feel like." Neither did He ask the people to bring 90 percent of their harvest. He knew we would need something to live on. But He did say, "Give Me a tenth."

Maybe God knew the Israelites would need help organizing their giving so He suggested that they get into the habit of giving something. Maybe He knew that if they were ever going to get around to giving, they needed to plan their giving.

I see tithing as a practical plan for giving my time as well. That means I don't need to take on the entire church sick list singlehandedly. But I can plan to adopt one person a week whom I call, visit, or contact in some special way. It doesn't mean I have to set up a crisis center in my home for all the hurting hearts in the congregation. Crisis situations take a great deal of time and emotional energy, and I know I cannot carry more than one stress load at a time. But I can reach out to one person in crisis and will be able to see that person through it because I'm not trying to carry too many burdens.

His job or our job? Each person must answer this for herself. But as far as I'm concerned, it's both. It is his job in terms of details, hours invested, amount of expertise, and physical participation. But it is our job in terms of feeling with, being interested in, asking about, listening to, observing, and supporting. To me that is the meaning of being "one flesh."

Interaction Time
Personal Reflection

1. A time I feel I was too involved in my husband's ministry was when. . . .

2. The way it affected our marriage was. . . .

3. A time I feel I was not involved enough in my husband's ministry was when. . . .

4. The way it affected our marriage was. . . .

5. If my husband and I talked today about my feelings toward my involvement in his ministry, I would say. . . .

6. If my husband and I talked today about my feelings toward my involvement in his ministry, I think *he* would say. . . .

7. In order to find out how my husband feels about my involvement with him in ministry, a question I might ask him is. . . .

8. When I have taken on too many commitments it shows up in the following ways. . . .

9. Right now I feel my commitment to church and my commitment to home (is, is not) in healthy balance.

10. If I do not feel in balance, a step I might need to take is. . . .

11. One reason I may have difficulty keeping home and church responsibilities in balance is. . . .

12. If I had to decide which area of my life receives the greatest amount of my time, I would have to say (temporary relationships—i.e., friends, congregational members, neighbors, clients, or permanent relationships—i.e., family).

13. I (am, am not) comfortable with this appropriation of my time.

14. Biblical principles that relate to the issue of maintaining balance and ordering priorities are. . . .

15. Scriptural references that support the principles are. . . .

16. My prayer for myself concerning balance and priorities is. . . .

Group Interaction
1. Some feel that if it is God's work, a pastor's wife should never say no when asked to serve. She should accept and trust God's supernatural strength to see her through the assignment. Do you agree or disagree? Why?

2. What do you think of the statement, "It's better to burn out than to rust out?" Do you think it is a good philosophy of life for the pastor's wife? Why or why not?

3. What have you found to be a helpful criterion in evaluating how involved to be in your husband's work?

4. What do you recommend for a pastoral couple who are not comfortable with their congregation's "two for the price of one" mentality?

5. How do you respond to the adage, "Both husband and wife are called to the ministry"?

6. If you agree that both must feel the call, how does "the call" work itself out practically for the pastor's wife?

7. How do you interpret "partners in ministry"? What has it meant in your marriage style?

8. How does the concept "partners in ministry" apply to the pastor's wife who is busily involved in her own career (or does it apply at all to her)? How might his job and her job fit happily together?

9. What would you say to the pastor's wife who remains detached from parish involvement and never accepts invitations to serve in her husband's church? Do you think in some situations she has legitimate reason? If so, what might some reasons be?

10. From God's point of view, what do you think "one flesh" means? Does a couple need to decide which one? Explain.

11. Share with the group one specific prayer request you have concerning maintaining balance in your life.

ELEVEN

Where Does Job End and Home Begin?
Learning to Maintain a Balance

Jeff didn't tell us everything about his past. He never talked much about his parents. But he had shared some of his feelings with us over cups of coffee or Sunday dinners. His parents were missionaries—some of the best among the crop of veterans. His father was considered an expert in his field and wrote insightful articles about understanding the ways of foreign cultures. His mother was a highly educated teacher and used her educational expertise to train those who otherwise would have no opportunities for learning.

Jeff came home to the States to go to high school. He floundered in the seas of the unknown. He moved in a world all his own and seldom let anyone else inside. One day I caught a glimpse when the door cracked open. I watched him run eagerly to his mailbox to look for a foreign postmark. There was none. He joked and laughed about it, but I felt he was hiding his disappointment.

Finally Jeff almost went under. His girlfriend was pregnant. His parents were heartbroken. Jeff resented their heartbreak. "Why is it they had time for everyone but me before this happened?" he asked. I could not answer him.

Gradually, I saw Jeff reject not only his parents, but the church which he felt had cheated him out of a mother and father. He resented the Christianity that made parents pour their time and talents into building up the people of God while their own families fell apart. Jeff's rehabilitation was long and hard. He still carries, and will probably always carry the scars— because a job was more important to his parents than he was.

I hear stories like Jeff's, and I fear. How do I know whether a job is becoming more important than a person? How much time spent with Mark and the children is enough time? How many date nights per month does it take to keep a marriage together? What kind of work schedule did the parents have who seem to have raised well-adjusted kids?

This is one of the many tensions in life that God didn't choose to solve for us. But He did give us examples and principles to assist us as we work through our own tensions. He also gave us two good eyes with which to observe and two good ears to hear what those closest to us sometimes try to tell us.

"Know what I like best about vacations," Jori asked as we relaxed by the motel pool on the first day of our vacation. "I like that we have our mommy and daddy all to ourselves." I knew what she meant. I knew that her innocent remark was not an indictment of her parents or of the church and the graduate school which kept them busy. But her candidness spoke volumes.

I have felt Jori's feelings. I've lived with myself long enough to know that I like to feel I am the most important person in the world to someone. If my family doesn't make me feel "number one," there is a good possibility I will never know the feeling. Everyone else is too involve : in their own world to offer me that kind of commitment. How tragic when someone has to go through life always playing second fiddle to someone or something else.

Giving that "number one" feeling to a person usually means that something or someone else will have to wait. If something else is always crowding my family out of my life, they soon know where they fit in my set of priorities. However, if I value my relationship with them, I will go to great trouble for them. I will say "I love you" not just with my words, but with the sacrifices I am willing to make for them.

That's what the Cross says to me: God says, "You are so important to Me that I will go to all the trouble of dying for you. I won't just write 'I love you' with My handwriting in the sky; I will make a sacrifice for you just to show you how important you are to Me." Without the Cross, God's love is just empty words.

One of the most powerful messages I've ever received was a message my dad gave to me. He often took me on his knee and said, "I love you." I knew the feel of his strong arms around me and his kisses on my cheek. But none of his expressions of love affected my life as much as the one he gave me when I was fifteen years old.

My dad had been in church work in the rural South for thirteen years. The joy of his life was to go into a little community that had no church and begin one. He was a gentle man, and people for miles around came to him because they knew him, loved him, and needed him.

However, one day he began to realize that his one and only daughter needed something the small country schools and the small rural churches were not providing for her. There were no Christian friends, no active youth groups. So my parents began to think in terms of the Pennsylvania urban center from which they had come thirteen years earlier.

They didn't ship me back East to live with relatives and go to school. Instead, they said good-bye to the work and the people they loved so much. They moved back East where churches and preachers were a dime a dozen. My dad drove a bread truck and then sold meat to feed our family of seven. He lost his churches, but he kept his daughter. He knew what sacrifice was all about. I have never been in doubt about what is the most important thing in my dad's life. And that has always been a secure, happy feeling for me.

The more I read about the life of Christ, the more impressed I am with His life of balance. He walked the balance beam with perfect precision. He developed mentally, spiritually, physically, and socially (Luke 2:52). And I believe that in all those compartments of His life He kept Himself from leaning too far in any one direction.

His example offers me insight into balancing my responsibility to other people and my responsibility to my family. I believe Jesus knew the balance between private and public. Sometimes He escaped into the mountains alone, and other times He mingled with the crowds. No doubt He knew when He needed both.

There is a time for me to reach out to people, and there is a time to close my doors to them so our family can be alone. Knowing whether the moment calls for a closed or an open door is not always easy.

Mark used to have a group of young single adults who worked with him on the Wednesday night youth programs at church. I got into the habit of inviting one or two of them over for dinner on Wednesday nights since most of them lived alone.

I didn't think twice about this particular dinner invitation. We went into our normal Wednesday evening routine: Mark came home. Our guests arrived. We sat down to eat. The children were at their worst. Our meal turned into chaos. Both children wanted Daddy's attention and pulled all sorts of stunts to get it; they spent a good part of the meal in their rooms.

Later that evening as I consoled a tearful Jori in her room after the commotion had died down and her daddy and friends had gone to church, she said, "But I haven't talked to my daddy for three whole days." I suddenly understood what had happened. Daddy was at church all day Sunday, out of town Monday, at a dinner/board meeting Tuesday night, and by Wednesday evening the children had three days worth of love and information to give him. That evening was not the night to have his attention divided between them and guests.

I'm all for having guests. I'm for having my children listen to adult conversations at the dinner table. I remember how much I learned about faraway lands from the missionaries who stayed in our home during missionary conferences, or how many pastors' jokes I learned from the traveling evangelists who spent a week in our home each year. I remember how I drooled over the neat college guys who stayed with us when they had concerts in our church.

I want our children to be exposed to people, and there is no better exposure than to have people stay in our home and eat at our table. But in my zeal for exposure or hospitality or for whatever reason I entertain, I must remember that there are times when our family needs to be alone. When I lean too much in one direction or the other, my family often gives me clues.

It was the end of a week of out-of-town guests. Nicky's room had been the guest room. He had slept on the floor beside our bed for the entire week. It had been great sport to him at first; he had been happy to give up nap time to see the sights of the city with us. He had eaten late, risen early, and slept whenever and wherever he could. On Friday morning, Nicky disappeared. We looked everywhere. No Nicky. Finally someone discovered him curled up under his bed with his blanket. When I tried to coax him out, his response was, "I don't want persons." He had had enough.

We all have times when we want to curl up under our bed and say, "I don't want persons." I don't see that as unchristian or selfish, unsociable or inhospitable. It doesn't mean I'm a pious recluse. I see it as acknowledging my humanness. Sometimes I need to crawl under and curl up. Sometimes I need peace and quiet. Sometimes my family needs the same. Jesus did not ignore that need in Himself.

Had Jesus lived in twentieth-century America, I believe He would have known what to do about His phone. I think He would have taken it off the hook at mealtime so He could listen to those who were closest to Him. I don't think He would have permitted Himself to become public property at the expense of time He needed to spend with His inner circle of twelve.

One of my friends, who happens to be a pastor's wife, used to spend hours each day on the phone listening to people talk about things they felt her husband should know but were afraid to go and tell him themselves. The easiest way to get to the pastor when you don't want to face him is to go through his wife, or so this congregation seemed to feel. And his wife always had a listening ear. She also had a very bad knot in her neck from using her head to hold the phone while she washed the dishes, ironed the clothes, sewed on buttons, scrubbed the kitchen floor, cooked the meals, and did anything else she could do within reach of her phone.

"There aren't many spots in my house I can't go with my phone," she said half-jokingly and half-desperately. She admitted that she knew more about that congregation than she ever needed to know or even cared to know. She had listened to enough information under the prayer-request label to keep her on her knees for five years. My friend finally concluded that she was about to choke herself on her own phone cord. She began to realize that there were times when she could best serve people by saying no to them.

I believe that in the demands of His world and in the press of His business, Jesus knew when to say no. I also believe He knew how much to do for others and how much to ask them to do for themselves. He mixed the clay and applied it to the blind man's eyes, but He asked the man to go himself and wash his eyes in the pool (John 9:1-7).

Sometimes in our business of serving others we may make ourselves leaning posts when we should be asking others to stand on their own. We may become sounding boards when we should be encouraging others to stop talking and start doing. We may give to others when we should provide the opportunity for them to give to us.

God doesn't expect us to walk the balance beam with perfect precision. He understands about the forces in our lives that keep pulling us toward the extreme. He knows that we can't juggle all the items in our lives so that they come down in proper order. Only one Man ever lived that way.

But God does offer us the potential for peaceful living. He knows we will be happier if our lives approach a state of equilibrium. "Happy are the peacemakers," Jesus said (Matt. 5:9, paraphrased). I believe Jesus knew we would need peace and order in our lives, externally and internally. Because He cared about the whole person, I believe He knew that our well-being depends on all the pieces of our lives fitting together into a proper perspective. I have confidence that peaceful, balanced living is possible because our God is not a God of confusion, but of peace (1 Cor. 14:33).

Interaction Time
Personal Reflection

1. A time my husband made me feel I was the most important person in the world to him was when. . . .

2. The result was. . . .

3. A time I attempted to make my children feel they were the most important people in the world to me was when. . . .

4. The result was. . . .

5. Clues my children give me when they are feeling crowded out of my life by my schedule or by other people are. . . .

6. I (am, am not) satisfied with the way I respond when my children give me clues they are not feeling like priorities to me.

7. When my children seem to feel secure about where they fit into Mother's list of priorities, they. . . .

8. True or false. Sometimes I imagine my children are feeling neglected when they are really not.

9. True or false. Sometimes I worry too much about whether I am spending enough time with my children.

10. True or false. Sometimes I am overly concerned that my children will grow up resenting the ministry because it deprived them of a mother and dad.

11. If my answer to the above three questions is true, I might need to . . .

12. How much time spent with your children is enough time? Someone I might talk to about this issue is. . . .

13. As far as I am concerned, the most important thing a pastor's wife can do for her children is. . . .

14. I (am, am not) satisfied that I am doing that for my children.

15. A verse in Scripture that is helpful when it comes to determining priorities is. . . .

Group Interaction
1. Do you think that it is possible for mothers to ever make their children too much of a priority? Explain.

2. Is it ever possible for a pastor's wife to use "family commitments" as a cop out? Explain.

3. If you were friends with a pastor's wife who seemed to be using family commitments as a cop-out, what would you advise her?

4. What would you advise a pastor's wife who is concerned that her husband (the pastor) is not spending enough time with his children?

5. What would you recommend if she feels she is not spending enough time with her children?

6. How does one know when time invested in direct involvement with children is enough time?

7. What is the best way for finding balance between time invested in outside commitments and time invested in family?

8. We have all heard stories from disillusioned pastors' kids who blame their parents' ministries for their disillusionment. How can a pastor's wife keep from becoming paranoid about that possibility?

9. What is the best advice you have ever received for keeping your life in balance when it comes to family and outside commitments?

10. What is the best advice you can think of that Jesus gave for maintaining balance?

11. How would you pray for a sister pastor's wife who is struggling in this area? Offer that prayer to God right now.

TWELVE

Life—a Pain or a Pleasure?
Learning about Positive Outlooks

"Happiness is not doing what you like but liking what you do," said Wally Phillips on one of our local morning radio programs. It was a cold, bleak, windy Chicago day. The prospects for the day were just about as gloomy as the weather—clean the house and shop for groceries. I called them drudgery days. The nerve of Wally Phillips to talk about happiness on a day like this! What he really said to me that morning was, "Cleaning your house and shopping for groceries are not drudgery. You make them drudgery."

Wally was right, though it was hard to admit. What life boils down to is my attitude toward it. It is not life that brings me boredom or happiness; my response makes the difference.

I can be in a honeymoon suite of the Ritz-Carlton on downtown Chicago's "Magnificent Mile" and still be miserable. Or I can be in my three-bedroom ranch, down on my hands and knees scrubbing the kitchen floor, and still be happy. Circumstances do not make me miserable or happy. I make myself miserable or happy.

The apostle Paul made a Wally Phillips type statement some 1900 years earlier. "It doesn't matter whether I'm rich or poor, full or hungry," Paul said, "I can be content in any circumstances" (Phil. 4:11-12, author's paraphrase). Paul knew that contentment was something he carried around with him in his heart, rather than a warm-fuzzy he extracted from his environment.

Paul could say "I'm content" even though he was sitting in prison, because his general feeling about his life and his God was one of contentment. No doubt because he was a contented person, when the prison experiences came along, his predisposition was toward contentment.

My general outlook on life will affect my specific responses to life. "When a man is gloomy, everything seems to go wrong. When he is cheerful, everything seems right," the writer of Proverbs observed (Prov. 15:15). If I am a gloomy person, I will respond gloomily to most situations. If I've cultivated negativism in my life, I will respond negatively to much of life. If, on the other hand, I've worked hard at being a cheerful person, my automatic reaction, even to gloomy situations, will be one of cheer.

That doesn't mean I'm some kind of robot that is programmed for cheerfulness only. I will have my gloomy days. There will be times when I *don't want to, don't care,* and *don't want to care.* We all have our moments of gloom. But there is a big difference between sporadic moments and permanent outlook.

Today's weather forecast calls for rain. The clouds are dark. But Chicago's climate is not rainy. Black clouds do not dominate our skies. There is a difference between today's weather and the general climatic conditions of our area.

The same is true with life: the weather makes the climate. If all my days are dark, dreary, and depressing, no doubt I will become a dark, dreary, and depressing person. If my life is sunny, with a few rainy days here and there, I'm more likely to develop into a sunshine-type person—one who is fun to be around.

An interesting thing about the climate of my life is that it's contagious. Happiness is catching. So is gloom. If I am not a happy person to be around, there is a good possibility that those around me won't be happy either. If I feel weighed down by the burdens and cares of life, no doubt those who are with me will feel weighed down by the burdens and cares of life.

I believe in sharing one another's burdens. The Bible tells me to do that (Gal. 6:2). And that means I have to be willing to let others carry my burdens with me. But it doesn't mean I have to manufacture burdens or make a burden out of a feather. Jesus talked about light burdens (Matt. 11:30). I think perhaps He meant that the burdens will be there, but how we carry them determines whether they are heavy or light.

Heavy-load-carrying people often make others think about how heavy their own load is. If someone begins to tell me all the things that are wrong in his or her life, I tend to find all kinds of things that are wrong about my life too. Maybe it's "misery loves company" at work, or maybe it's my way of letting them know I'm feeling with them. At any rate, we both end up sitting around in the mud puddles of life and feeling sorry for each other.

God must have made mud puddles for some reason, but I'm sure it wasn't for us to sit in them. I'm convinced that life is too short for sitting in mud puddles and feeling sorry for ourselves. Sitting in mud puddles all day is also a good way to catch cold. Proverbs tells me that happiness is good for my health! "A cheerful heart is good medicine, but a crushed spirit dries up the bones. Pleasant words are a honeycomb, sweet to the soul and healing to the bones" (Prov. 17:22; 16:24).

One thing that makes a difference in how I view my own situation is how I look at other's situations. If I think the grass is always greener just over the fence, I will be dissatisfied with my side of the fence. It's easy to fantasize that my life would be much happier if I were married to a different man, or if my husband had a different job, or if we lived in a different part of the country. The thing I forget is that any other man would have his faults; any other job would have its snags; any other part of the country would have its bad-weather days. Things always look glamorous from faraway. It's when we get up close that we can see the blemishes.

I had an acquaintance tell me that she hated every minute of being a pastor's wife. She felt that things would be much improved if her husband got out of the ministry and into business. "The pressures in the pastorate are just too great," she said. I talked with her again not very long ago. Her husband left his pastorate five years ago. Now she is having a difficult time accepting the pressures of the business world.

There are some things about being a pastor's wife that I don't like. It has its disadvantages. One is the long hours. Sometimes I find them hard to take. But I like the approach of one of my neighbors whose husband was a professional musician and traveled 90 percent of the time. "I decided long ago that I'd rather have Chuck part-time than anyone else full-time," Sally told me one day when I asked her if having an absentee husband didn't bother her.

Any job has its negatives. But the positives are there if I look for them. I've found some advantages in Mark's job: I like to be with people; Mark's job includes lots of people whom I have the opportunity of learning to know; I don't have to understand nuclear fission or computer science to understand exactly what Mark does; I don't have to schedule a walking tour of the plant for the kids and I to visit where daddy works; I'm able to see America and lands beyond—not many pastors' wives are left behind when their husbands tour a mission field or visit the Holy Land. One of my neighbors sat home alone last month for three weeks while her husband got an all-expense-paid trip to Japan. International Harvester didn't think about sending wives too.

I believe that our accomplishments in life are directly related to our outlook on life. Proverbs says, "As a man thinks within himself so he is" (Prov. 23:7). If I think discontentment, I will live a discontented life. If I think failure, I will probably never succeed. If I think I cannot, I probably never will. Paul said, "I can do everything through Him who gives me strength" (Phil. 4:13). And Paul did amazing things.

Not long ago I met a woman who should be the most depressed person around. Everything about her life that could possibly go wrong has, beginning with her childhood. She has every reason to be bitter and maladjusted. "Sometimes I laugh," she says. "Sometimes I cry. But God and I, we'll make it." I'm convinced they will. She and God are in the process of doing just that. She has used the hurts of her life to minister to those with similar hurts. She has instilled her hopefulness in countless others who have reason to despair. Every time I'm with her, I go away feeling, "God and I, we can make it too, even with all my flops and failures, my hurts and heartaches."

The story is told of an old Scottish fisherman who was having afternoon tea with some friends in a little tearoom by the sea. As he was describing some of his fishing exploits of the day, his hand accidentally knocked over his cup of tea. An ugly, brown tea stain appeared on the freshly whitewashed wall beside him.

"Never mind about the stain," said a friend as he rose from his chair and drew from his pocket a brown crayon. There emerged from that ugly, brown tea stain a magnificent stag with antlers spread and back arched. The friend of the fisherman was one of England's most famous painters.

Life is full of ugly tea stains that splash against whitewashed walls. Reality often seems to be more obstacle than opportunity, more pain than pleasure, more chaos than calm, more hurt than happiness, more tension than tenderness. But if I interpret Romans 8:28 correctly, I must believe that as God's woman, God is using everything in my life to make me more like Himself.

Together, He and I can take the tea stains in my life and make something out of them. We can take the chaos and be calm, take the tensions and be tender, take the hurts and be content, take the obstacles and build opportunities. That is what God offers me from life.

And when God says that's what He can do for me, only my unbelief keeps me from experiencing it. If the Christian life is worth living, then God is worth believing. And if I believe God, there is no end to the possibilities.

Interaction Time
Personal Reflection

1. If someone asked me to describe myself in terms of positive outlook or negative outlook toward ministry, I'd say. . . .

2. My initial response to a situation in the church tends to be (positive, negative).

3. True or False. I usually imagine the worst.

4. True or False. I am much more likely to pick up on what is wrong about the ministry than I am to pick up on what is right about it.

5. The way my outlook on the ministry could affect our children is. . . .

6. The way my outlook on the ministry could affect the people in our congregation is. . . .

7. If there is anything I would like to change about my outlook on ministry it is. . . .

8. One bonus of the ministry for me has been. . . .

9. The last positive statement I've made to my husband about being in the ministry was. . . .

10. The last positive statement I've made to my children about their daddy being in the ministry was. . . .

11. My prayer about maintaining a positive outlook for ministry would be. . . .

12. My advice to someone who is struggling with a negative outlook toward ministry would be. . . .

Group Interaction

1. How can you recognize a pastor's wife who is unhappy about her husband's being in the ministry?

2. In comparison, how can you recognize a pastor's wife who is happy about her husband's being in the ministry?

3. In what ways does a negative spirit contaminate?

4. What might you say to a pastor's wife who blames the ministry for her struggles?

5. How does one go about developing a positive outlook?

6. Share an experience you have had where your negative spirit worked against you.

7. Share an experience you have had where your positive spirit worked for you.

8. What made the difference?

9. If you were having difficulty being positive about your situation as a pastor's wife, what verses from Scripture might be helpful?

10. What examples from Scripture might be helpful? (See for example, the Psalms and David's example of positiveness in the midst of tense situations or Paul's example from the book of Philippians.)

11. If you were praying for someone who was having trouble being positive about her situation as a pastor's wife, what would you ask God to do for her? Go around your group and pray for one another concerning this issue.